A Child's First Library of Learning

Where Things Come From

TIME-LIFE BOOKS • ALEXANDRIA, VIRGINIA

Contents

? Where Do Blue Jeans Come From?

ANSWER Blue jeans are made from fluffy cotton, which grows on plants. The first blue jeans were sewn from a cotton cloth called denim by a man named Levi Strauss. He sold them to goldminers in California, who needed extra-strong work pants.

1. Big, noisy machines pick raw, white cotton from the fields. The cotton grows in rounded seed pods, called bolls.

2. The cotton is washed carefully to get rid of seeds, stems, and insects. It is then rolled into cotton "logs."

3. The cotton fibers are spun and twisted tight, making thread that is not much different from the kind used to sew on buttons.

4. Blue jeans get their blue color when the cotton thread is plunged into a tub of blue dye.

4

▶ 5. A machine called a loom weaves many threads together, making denim cloth. Look closely at your jeans and you will see the little threads that make up the material.

▶ 6. An electric saw cuts the denim into panels, or pieces. This saw can cut through 120 layers of denim at one time.

▶ 7. Workers sew the denim panels together, making a pair of blue jeans just the right size for you.

MINI-DATA

The first jeans had to hold a goldminer's heavy tools. Copper rivets, or pins, were added to make the pockets stronger.

When kids started wearing jeans to school, teachers complained that the rivets on the back pockets damaged the school's chairs. That's why there are no rivets on your back pockets today.

● To the Parent

Denim has not always been blue—nor has it always been used to make jeans. The material was originally used to make white sails. A group of sailors from Genoa discovered that the denim in their sails made good material for a pair of pants. People dubbed these sailor-made trousers "genes" after the Genoese seafarers who wore them.

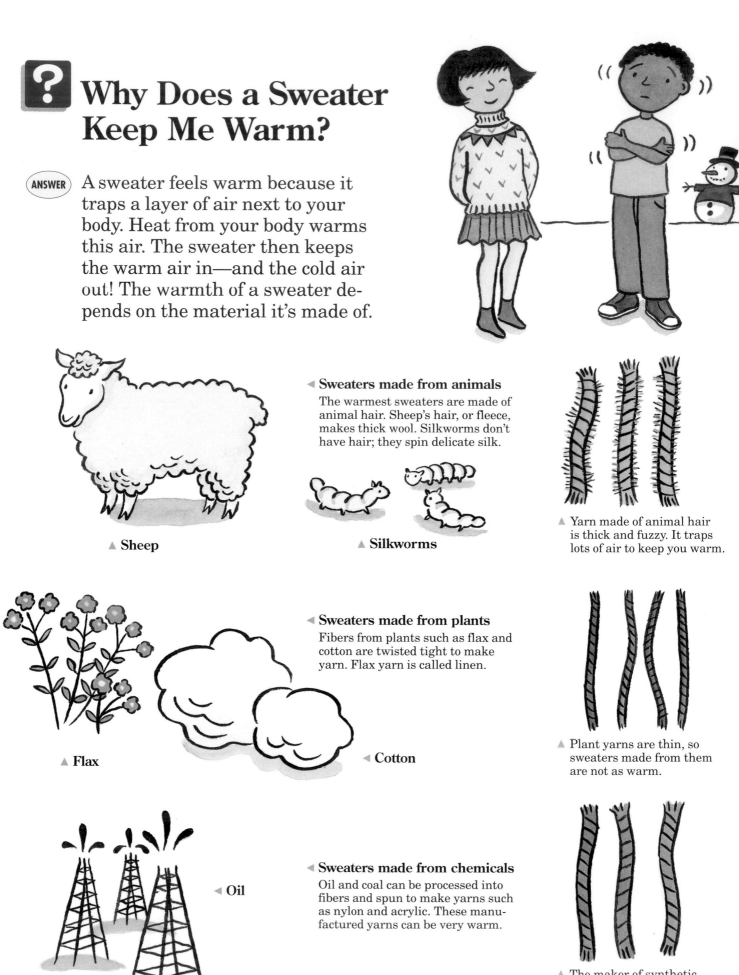

? Why Does a Sweater Keep Me Warm?

ANSWER A sweater feels warm because it traps a layer of air next to your body. Heat from your body warms this air. The sweater then keeps the warm air in—and the cold air out! The warmth of a sweater depends on the material it's made of.

◄ **Sweaters made from animals**
The warmest sweaters are made of animal hair. Sheep's hair, or fleece, makes thick wool. Silkworms don't have hair; they spin delicate silk.

▲ **Sheep**

▲ **Silkworms**

▲ Yarn made of animal hair is thick and fuzzy. It traps lots of air to keep you warm.

◄ **Sweaters made from plants**
Fibers from plants such as flax and cotton are twisted tight to make yarn. Flax yarn is called linen.

▲ **Flax**

◄ **Cotton**

▲ Plant yarns are thin, so sweaters made from them are not as warm.

◄ **Oil**

◄ **Sweaters made from chemicals**
Oil and coal can be processed into fibers and spun to make yarns such as nylon and acrylic. These manufactured yarns can be very warm.

▲ The maker of synthetic yarns decides how thick or thin the fibers will be.

How Is Yarn Made into a Sweater?

No matter what it's made of, yarn must be woven into fabric to make a sweater. This is usually done by knitting. A knitting machine, or a person who knits, hooks rows of wavy yarn to each other, making fabric. The fabric pieces are then sewn together to create a sweater.

▲ This pattern is usually on the outside of a knitted sweater. Can you find it on yours?

▲ This pattern is often on the inside of your sweater. You can see how the wavy rows are locked together.

● **To the Parent**

T-shirts, sweatpants, socks, and scarves are all knitted garments. Examine these items closely and you may be able to distinguish the interlocking loops of yarn that indicate the fabric is a knit. Not all sweaters are knitted; some may be crocheted or woven. Learning to crochet is a fun and manageable craft project for young children.

How Are Sneakers Made?

ANSWER Making a pair of sneakers is a complicated job. That's because a sneaker may have as many as 20 different parts, and each one must be made and attached separately. In a good sneaker, the parts work together to keep your foot safe and comfortable while you run and play.

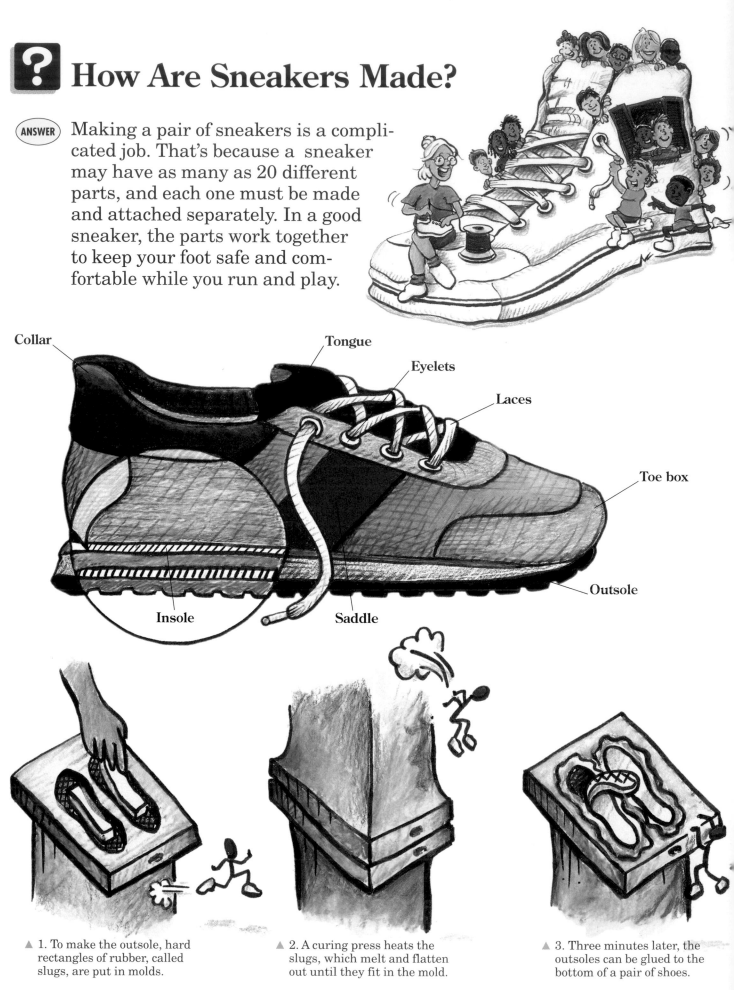

Collar

Tongue

Eyelets

Laces

Toe box

Insole

Saddle

Outsole

▲ 1. To make the outsole, hard rectangles of rubber, called slugs, are put in molds.

▲ 2. A curing press heats the slugs, which melt and flatten out until they fit in the mold.

▲ 3. Three minutes later, the outsoles can be glued to the bottom of a pair of shoes.

8

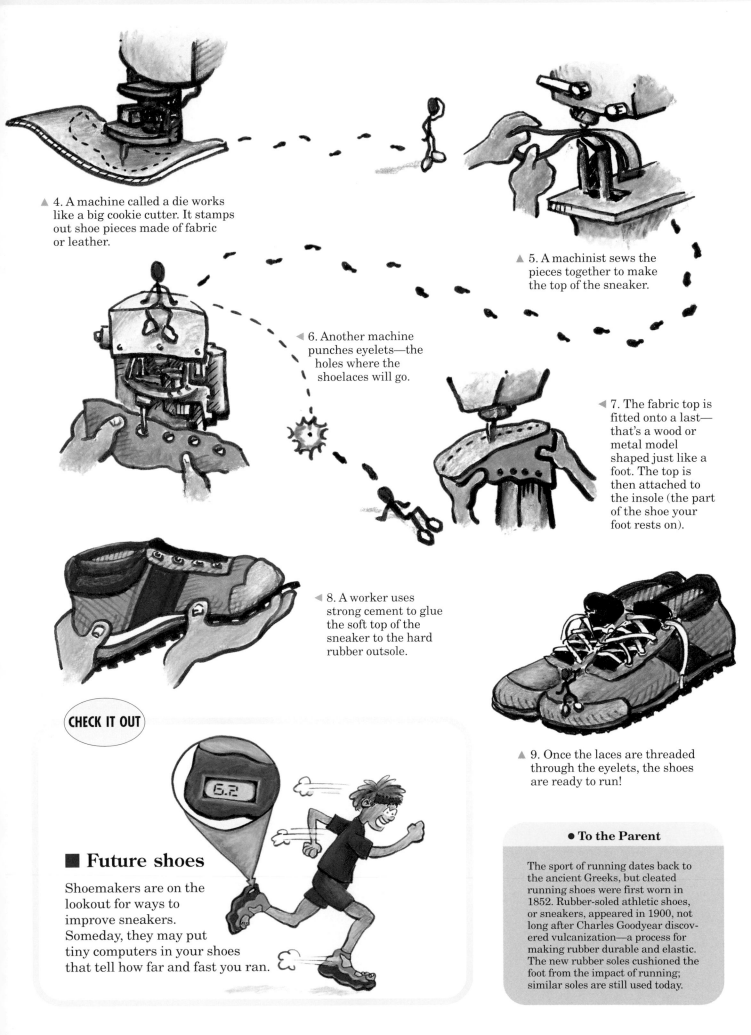

▲ 4. A machine called a die works like a big cookie cutter. It stamps out shoe pieces made of fabric or leather.

▲ 5. A machinist sews the pieces together to make the top of the sneaker.

◀ 6. Another machine punches eyelets—the holes where the shoelaces will go.

◀ 7. The fabric top is fitted onto a last— that's a wood or metal model shaped just like a foot. The top is then attached to the insole (the part of the shoe your foot rests on).

◀ 8. A worker uses strong cement to glue the soft top of the sneaker to the hard rubber outsole.

▲ 9. Once the laces are threaded through the eyelets, the shoes are ready to run!

CHECK IT OUT

■ Future shoes

Shoemakers are on the lookout for ways to improve sneakers. Someday, they may put tiny computers in your shoes that tell how far and fast you ran.

● To the Parent

The sport of running dates back to the ancient Greeks, but cleated running shoes were first worn in 1852. Rubber-soled athletic shoes, or sneakers, appeared in 1900, not long after Charles Goodyear discovered vulcanization—a process for making rubber durable and elastic. The new rubber soles cushioned the foot from the impact of running; similar soles are still used today.

❓ How Are Crayons Made?

ANSWER Two main ingredients go into a crayon. They are paraffin wax—the same sort of wax used in candles—and powdered pigments, which give crayons their color. These two ingredients are mixed to make crayons in 104 colors.

▲ 1. Dry pigments can be used on their own or mixed to make other colors.

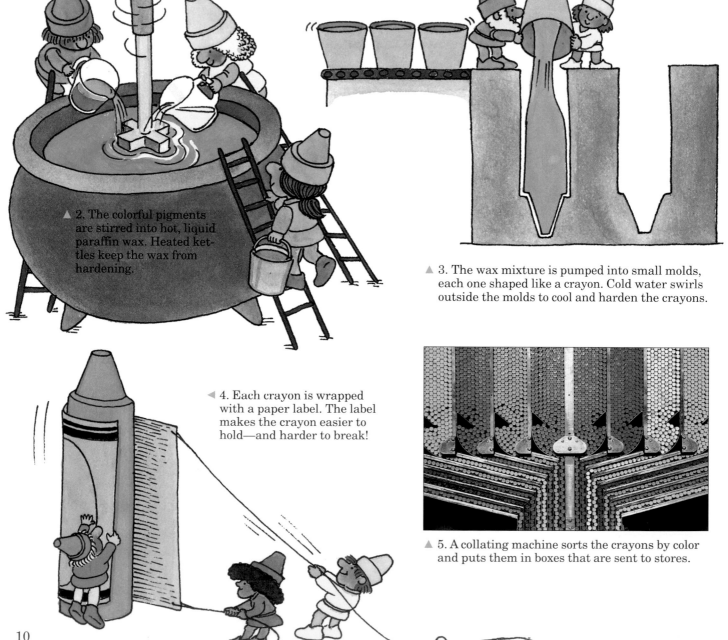

▲ 2. The colorful pigments are stirred into hot, liquid paraffin wax. Heated kettles keep the wax from hardening.

▲ 3. The wax mixture is pumped into small molds, each one shaped like a crayon. Cold water swirls outside the molds to cool and harden the crayons.

◄ 4. Each crayon is wrapped with a paper label. The label makes the crayon easier to hold—and harder to break!

▲ 5. A collating machine sorts the crayons by color and puts them in boxes that are sent to stores.

■ Bingo is her name-o

Bingo is a talented dog! Standing on her hind legs and holding a large crayon between her front paws, Bingo—a nine-year-old mixed breed—draws pictures such as the one shown here. According to Bingo's owner, Shirley Woodford, the artistic pooch can even pick out crayons of a certain color in response to voice commands.

■ Favorite colors

A survey conducted by the makers of Crayola crayons found that red and blue tied for first place as kids' favorite colors for crayons. Green came in second. What's *your* favorite crayon color?

? Is Pencil Lead Really Lead?

ANSWER Pencil leads look like the gray metal called lead, but that's not what they're made of. Pencil leads are a mixture of clay and graphite (a soft, black rock that people used to think was lead). Like diamonds and coal, graphite is made from carbon.

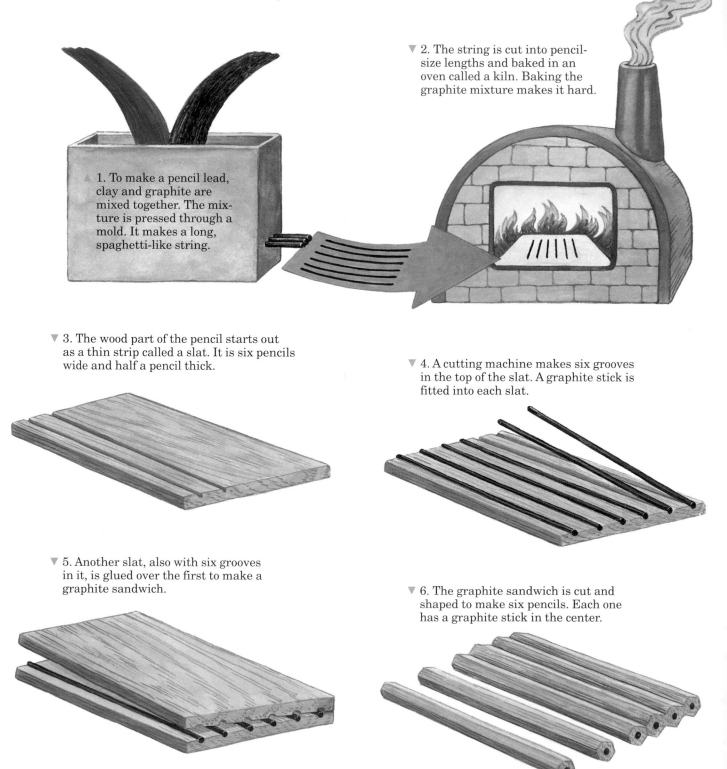

▼ 2. The string is cut into pencil-size lengths and baked in an oven called a kiln. Baking the graphite mixture makes it hard.

▲ 1. To make a pencil lead, clay and graphite are mixed together. The mixture is pressed through a mold. It makes a long, spaghetti-like string.

▼ 3. The wood part of the pencil starts out as a thin strip called a slat. It is six pencils wide and half a pencil thick.

▼ 4. A cutting machine makes six grooves in the top of the slat. A graphite stick is fitted into each slat.

▼ 5. Another slat, also with six grooves in it, is glued over the first to make a graphite sandwich.

▼ 6. The graphite sandwich is cut and shaped to make six pencils. Each one has a graphite stick in the center.

■ A crumby eraser

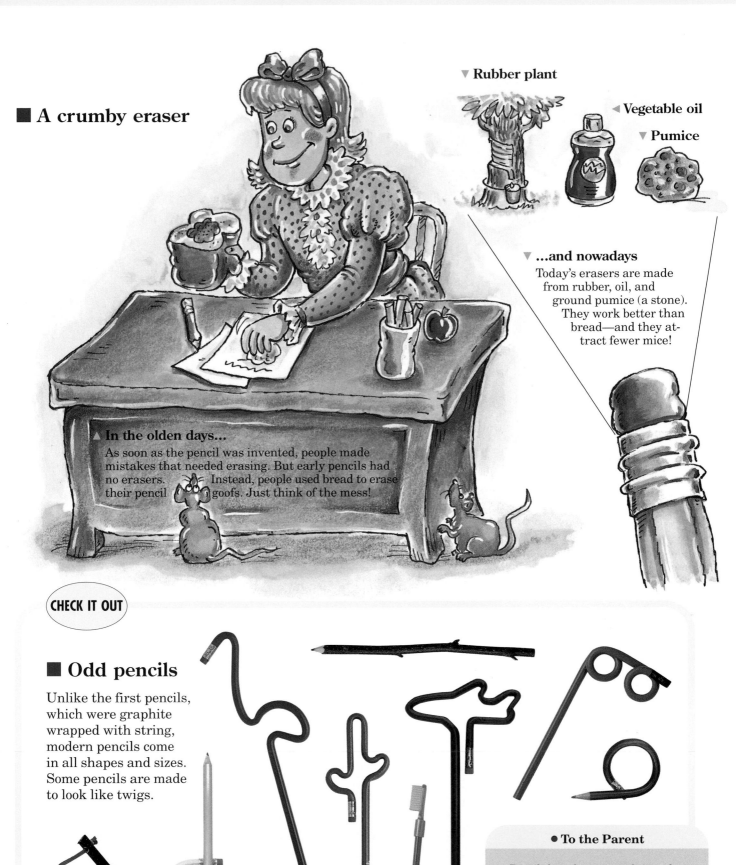

▼ **Rubber plant**

◀ **Vegetable oil**

▼ **Pumice**

▼ **...and nowadays**
Today's erasers are made from rubber, oil, and ground pumice (a stone). They work better than bread—and they attract fewer mice!

▲ **In the olden days...**
As soon as the pencil was invented, people made mistakes that needed erasing. But early pencils had no erasers. Instead, people used bread to erase their pencil goofs. Just think of the mess!

CHECK IT OUT

■ Odd pencils

Unlike the first pencils, which were graphite wrapped with string, modern pencils come in all shapes and sizes. Some pencils are made to look like twigs.

● To the Parent

Pencils have been around since the first graphite deposit was discovered by English farmers in 1564, but the rubber eraser wasn't invented until 1770. Even then, pencils and erasers were not paired up right away. Not until 1858 did an American inventor, Hyman Lipman, top things off by attaching an eraser to a pencil. Lipman sold his patent 14 years later for $100,000.

13

? Why Does Chalk Make So Much Dust?

ANSWER Chalk is dusty because it's made from powdered stone. The chalk you use for drawing on the sidewalk started out as a giant rock called limestone. Limestone rocks can be cut and then ground into a fine powder. So all that dust you see when you clean the erasers at school is really a cloud of limestone.

▶ **Grinding the rocks**
A big grinding machine smashes the limestone, making thr rock as fine as baby powder.

▲ **Mining the stone**
Workers cut limestone from a quarry—a deep pit with rock walls. Sometimes they use dynamite to make rocks small enough to carry.

▼ **Baking the chalk**
The clay is shaped into sticks, and the sticks are baked in an oven until they are hard— about four days.

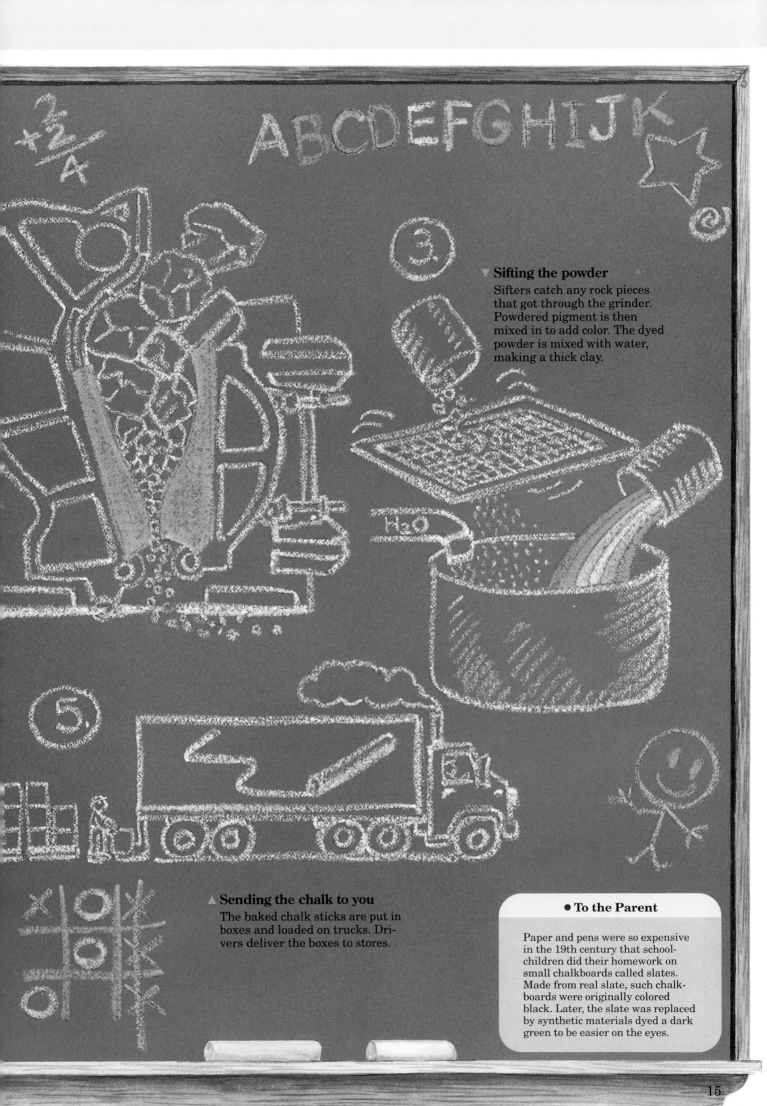

Sifting the powder

Sifters catch any rock pieces that got through the grinder. Powdered pigment is then mixed in to add color. The dyed powder is mixed with water, making a thick clay.

H_2O

Sending the chalk to you

The baked chalk sticks are put in boxes and loaded on trucks. Drivers deliver the boxes to stores.

Why Do We Recycle Paper?

(ANSWER) People recycle paper for many reasons. Recycling makes less trash; it also saves energy. Most important, recycling can save forests. Each year, 850 million trees are cut down and made into paper. Recycling lets some of those trees live to old age.

► **Paper recipe: Start with trees**
Lumber companies cut down trees and take them to a paper mill. There, the bark is stripped from the trunks. The trees are chopped into woodchips about one inch square.

Woodchips   Bleach   Recycled paper

► **Beat to a pulp**
The woodchips are mashed into a fine pulp. Chemicals that make paper stronger are added to this pulp; recycled paper is added, too. Finally, bleach is poured in to turn the paper white.

► **Spread on a web**
The wet pulp is spread over the top of a wire screen, called a web, that is 30 feet wide.

16

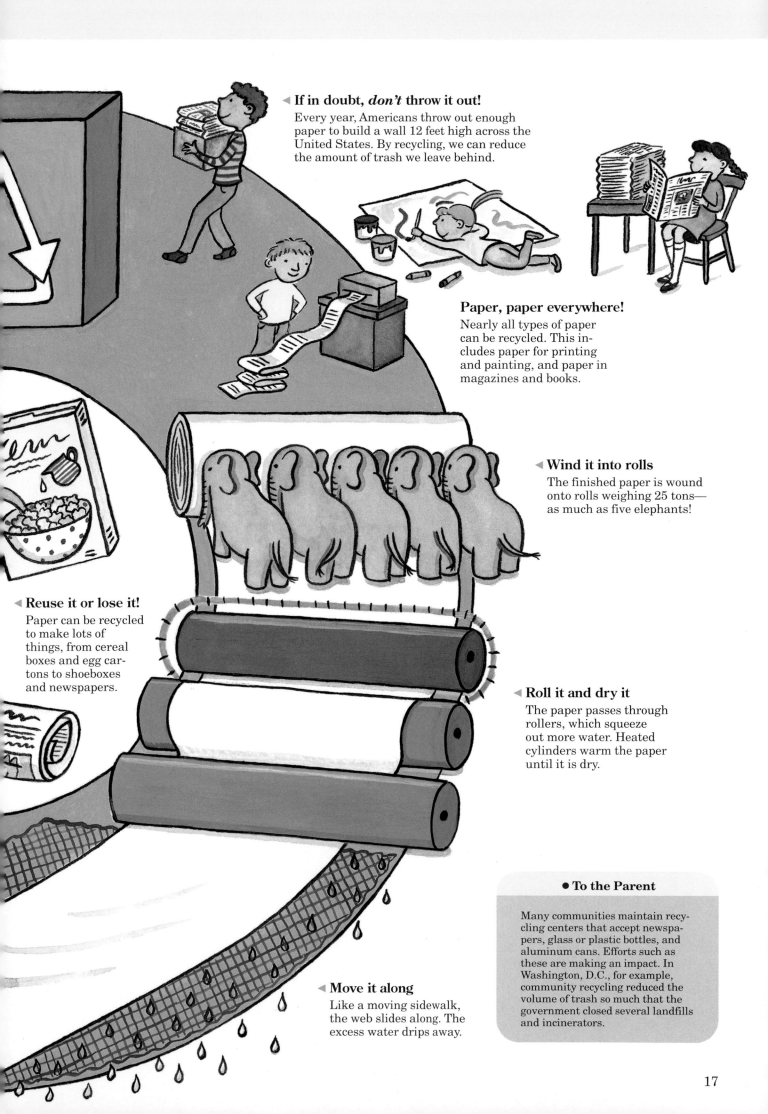

If in doubt, *don't* throw it out!

Every year, Americans throw out enough paper to build a wall 12 feet high across the United States. By recycling, we can reduce the amount of trash we leave behind.

Paper, paper everywhere!

Nearly all types of paper can be recycled. This includes paper for printing and painting, and paper in magazines and books.

Wind it into rolls

The finished paper is wound onto rolls weighing 25 tons— as much as five elephants!

Reuse it or lose it!

Paper can be recycled to make lots of things, from cereal boxes and egg cartons to shoeboxes and newspapers.

Roll it and dry it

The paper passes through rollers, which squeeze out more water. Heated cylinders warm the paper until it is dry.

Move it along

Like a moving sidewalk, the web slides along. The excess water drips away.

● To the Parent

Many communities maintain recycling centers that accept newspapers, glass or plastic bottles, and aluminum cans. Efforts such as these are making an impact. In Washington, D.C., for example, community recycling reduced the volume of trash so much that the government closed several landfills and incinerators.

How Do Cartoon Characters Come to Life?

ANSWER Cartoons are just drawings until animation brings them to life. To make a character move, an artist must first draw a series of pictures. Each picture looks just a little bit different from the one before it. When these pictures go by quickly, it looks as if the character is animated, or moving.

▲ 1. Making a storyboard is the first step in bringing a cartoon to life. Sketches on the storyboard show what the characters will do; words tell what they will say.

▲ 2. Actors record the words, and musicians record the music, that will become the cartoon's sound.

▲ 3. Artists known as master animators draw "key drawings" for each scene in the cartoon. The key drawings show the most important actions in every scene.

It takes 24 drawings to make one second of an animated movie. That means 43,200 drawings are in a half-hour cartoon. Working alone, you'd have to draw a picture a day for 118 years!

■ Hey, Walt Jr.!

The first cartoons were picture books called flip books. When the pages were flipped very fast, the pictures seemed to move. Try using a flip book to make your own cartoon!

Here's what you will need:

Pad of paper

Pencil or colored pens

▲ 1. On the *last* page of the flip book, draw a stick figure.

▲ 2. Turn one page and redraw the figure, changing it slightly.

▲ 3. Repeat step 2 until you get to the first page of the pad.

▲ 4. Flip the pages from bottom to top and enjoy the show!

4. Assistant animators draw the small movements, known as "in-betweens," that link one key drawing to the next.

5. The drawings are put onto thin celluloid sheets, called cels. Artists outline the drawings and color them in.

◄ 6. Each cel is photographed as a single frame. The frames are joined as a reel of film, which is fed through a projector. Light shines through the film onto a screen, where the pictures appear to be moving.

● **To the Parent**

Many modern animated films are made the traditional way, with artists drawing each cel by hand. More and more, however, the trend is toward computer-generated animation. *Toy Story* was the first feature film to be completely computer-animated.

? Where Do Pictures on TV Come From?

ANSWER The pictures on your television can come from anywhere in the world—and even from the moon! Most TV shows are filmed in studios, or buildings where actors perform in front of TV cameras. The cameras turn the pictures they take into electrical signals. These signals are then sent through wires or through the air to reach the TV set in your home.

■ Bringing the circus to you

▲ **At the studio**
A TV camera takes moving pictures of the action in a studio. It turns the pictures into electrical impulses, called signals.

▲ **Transmission center**
The TV signals go to a transmission center. The center sends them to your TV in one of three ways:

1. Through cable underground
If you have cable TV, the signals move along buried wires to your TV.

3. Through space

A satellite orbiting the earth can pick up TV signals. It sends them to a satellite dish that is connected by a cable to your TV.

■ Color TV

The picture on a TV screen is made of many tiny dots, or pixels. A pixel has only three colors: red, green, and blue. Your eye mixes the colors to see all the colors of a rainbow.

Red   **Green**   **Blue**

▼ To make white

When you see white on TV, pixels of all colors are lit.

▼ To make red

To make the color red, only the red pixels light up.

2. Through the air

Some TV signals travel invisibly through the air from tall transmission towers. A rooftop antenna picks up the signals and sends them to the TV along thin wires in your house.

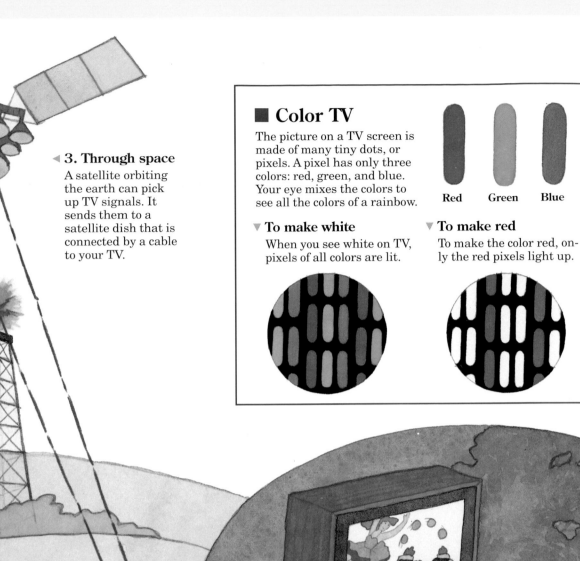

● To the Parent

A television camera takes 30 still pictures per second. When shown in rapid succession on a TV screen, these pictures cannot be distinguished as separate images by the eyes. The television picture thus seems to be moving continuously.

How Does a CD Make Music?

ANSWER A compact disk, or CD, is like a computer disk. It holds millions of little bits of information. Your CD player uses a laser—a narrowly focused beam of light—to read data stored on the disk. Inside the CD player is a computer, which turns that information into music.

◄ **Feelin' groovy**
1. Etched into the shiny side of a CD is a single track in the form of a long, spiral groove. The track contains tiny notches, or pits. In between the pits are flat surfaces.

▼ **A musical chip**
3. A computer chip turns the light-reader's information into music. It sends the music over wires to the speakers.

► **Reading laser light**
2. A beam of laser light hits the pits and flat areas, which reflect the light in a pattern. A light-reader turns this pattern into data that a computer can read.

Speakers of the house party

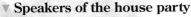

4. The speakers amplify the music—that means they make it loud enough for you to hear. If it's too loud, you're too old!

■ Miles of music

In order to hold all that music, the spiral track on a CD is three miles long! Spinning 200 to 500 times a minute, the disk can play 74 minutes of music without stopping.

FINISH

START

▶ A hair from your head is 60 times wider than the track on a compact disk.

● To the Parent

With more than one million bits of data used to produce a single second of CD sound, a standard computer disk would be able to hold less than three seconds of digital audio. This superior carrying capacity makes the compact disk an ideal storage medium for music, movies, and computer programs.

Where Does the Information on the Internet Come From?

From companies
The Internet isn't just for information; it's for fun, too! On the 'net, you can play games, look at pictures, or listen to music.

From experts
You can talk to all sorts of scientists on the 'net—even if they're in Antarctica. One group of students talked to space-shuttle astronauts while the crew was in space!

From screen pals
Electronic mail, or e-mail, is another way of sending information over the Internet.

From libraries
The Internet holds all sorts of information—even books! There's plenty to read in libraries and bookstores on line.

ANSWER It comes from everywhere! The Internet is made up of computers all over the world. These computers are linked by a worldwide "spider web" of wires. The main purpose of the Internet is for people to share information. That means anyone with a computer—even you—can put information on the 'net!

From encyclopedias

Does your teacher want a report on Australian emus? Search the 'net for photos, words, or even movies to help.

▲ **From old friends**

If a friend moves too far away to come over, you can play a game with that person over the Internet.

◄ **From the ends of the earth**

With the Internet spanning the globe, every continent is hooked up. Even the South Pole has its own connection.

(**CHECK IT OUT**)

■ Say it with a smilie

People on the Internet often use punctuation marks to communicate quickly. Called smilies, these funny symbols tell others what you're thinking.

:-) Smile!
:-D That's funny!
;-) Wink, wink
:-(How sad!
:'-(I'm crying
(-: I'm left-handed
8-) I wear glasses
8:-) I'm a girl
:-# I wear braces
!-O Yawn!
:-P Nyah, nyah!
:-X My lips are sealed
:-o What a surprise!
[] Hugs!
:-* Kisses!
---<--<(@ Here's a rose for you!

From new friends

With a computer and an Internet connection, you can make new friends anywhere in the world.

● **To the Parent**

The Internet started at UCLA in 1969 with a single node, or host computer. Named ARPANET after the Pentagon's Advanced Research Projects Agency, it was designed to be a fail-safe network whose decentralized structure would keep it running even if part of it was destroyed. In 1990, ARPANET gave way to the public Internet, which boasted 10 million hosts by 1997.

25

Where Does Cereal Come From?

ANSWER The cereal you ate for breakfast this morning traveled a long way to reach your table! Cereals are made from the seeds of special grasses, called grains. The grains most often used to make breakfast cereals are wheat, oats, and corn. A farmer grows the grain in a field, cuts it down, and sends it to a cereal factory. There the grain is cooked and formed into special shapes, then put in boxes and sent to stores.

Oats

Wheat

Corn

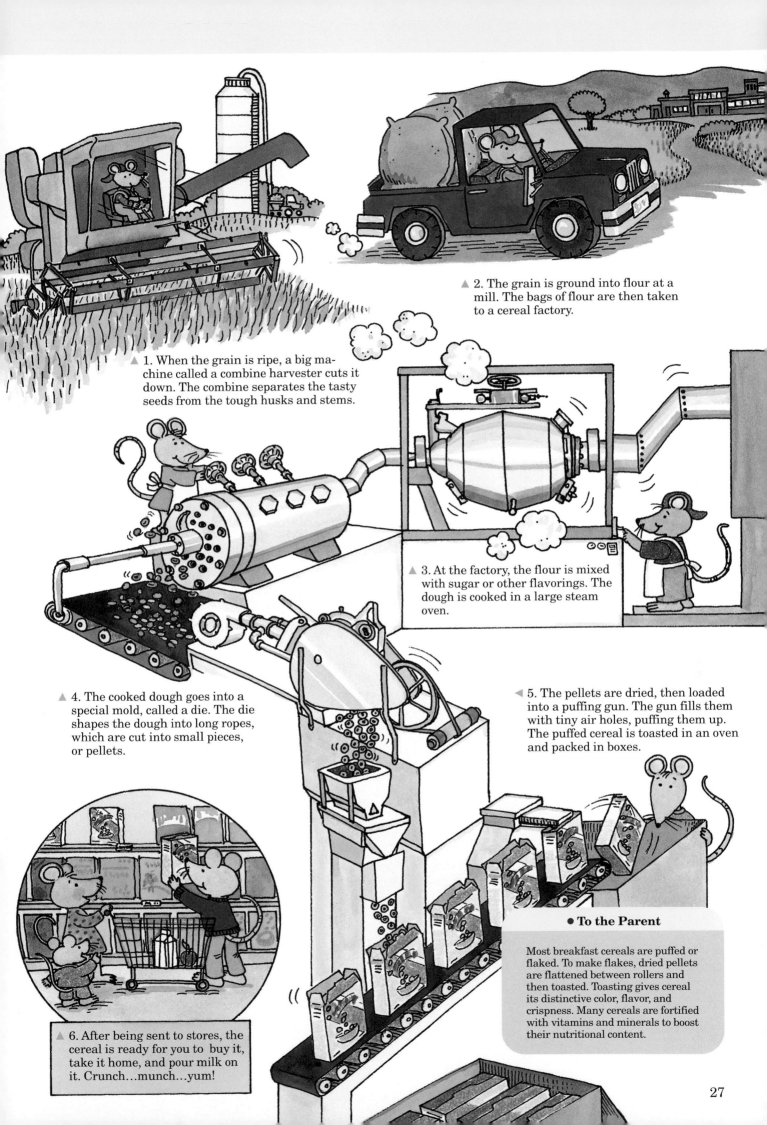

▲ 2. The grain is ground into flour at a mill. The bags of flour are then taken to a cereal factory.

▲ 1. When the grain is ripe, a big machine called a combine harvester cuts it down. The combine separates the tasty seeds from the tough husks and stems.

▲ 3. At the factory, the flour is mixed with sugar or other flavorings. The dough is cooked in a large steam oven.

▲ 4. The cooked dough goes into a special mold, called a die. The die shapes the dough into long ropes, which are cut into small pieces, or pellets.

◀ 5. The pellets are dried, then loaded into a puffing gun. The gun fills them with tiny air holes, puffing them up. The puffed cereal is toasted in an oven and packed in boxes.

● **To the Parent**

Most breakfast cereals are puffed or flaked. To make flakes, dried pellets are flattened between rollers and then toasted. Toasting gives cereal its distinctive color, flavor, and crispness. Many cereals are fortified with vitamins and minerals to boost their nutritional content.

▲ 6. After being sent to stores, the cereal is ready for you to buy it, take it home, and pour milk on it. Crunch…munch…yum!

Does All Salt Come from the Sea?

(ANSWER) No, it comes from shakers—just kidding!
Salt is found deep under the ground in hard,
thick layers called rock salt. These layers
were left behind when the salty water of
prehistoric oceans dried up, or evaporated.
Over time, the rock salt got buried by layers
of soil. Today, it has to be dug up.

▶ Millions of years ago,
oceans covered much
of the land that is now
dry. Then, as earth's
surface slowly shifted
about, large pools of
seawater got trapped
in lakes or ponds.

▲ The trapped seawater dried up, leaving
salt in its place. But the land kept moving,
so layers of earth buried the salt.

▶ To remove the under-
ground salt today, miners
pump water down into it.
The salt dissolves into a
liquid called brine, which
is pumped up to the sur-
face. The brine is boiled
until only salt is left.

■ What about sugar?

Sugar can be made from cane or beets, but the white sugar that is made from each plant looks and tastes the same. Brown sugar is white sugar that has been colored with molasses.

► Sugar cane

◄ Sugar beet

▲ **1. Hot and sweet sauce**
The cane or beets are crushed or chopped to make a sugary juice. The juice is then boiled down.

▲ **2. A positive spin**
A machine called a centrifuge spins the juice around. This separates the juice into syrup and small lumps of sugar called crystals. The thick, dark syrup spun off from cane sugar is molasses.

◄ Molasses

▲ Sugar

CHECK IT OUT

▲ **Sugar crystals**

▲ **Salt crystals**

Can you tell salt and sugar apart without tasting them? It's easy if you use a magnifying glass. Sugar crystals are longer, with slanted ends. Salt crystals look like cubes.

● **To the Parent**

Seawater is salty because rivers carry dissolved sodium and chlorine from the land to the ocean. The oldest method of harvesting salt—by evaporating seawater—is still in use. In hot, dry climates, seawater is trapped in large evaporation ponds. The resulting salt is known as sea salt.

Where Does Milk Come From?

ANSWER Most milk comes from cows, who turn grass into milk in three days. That sounds like magic—until you learn that a cow has four stomachs to do the job! At first the cow feeds the milk to her baby, called a calf. When the calf is three or four days old, the farmer starts milking the cow for milk that people can drink. One cow can make enough milk in a single day to fill 160 drinking glasses!

■ An udder success

A cow swallows grass without chewing it. The grass goes into her first and second stomachs, which break it into lumps called cuds. Later, the stomach muscles send the cuds back up to the cow's mouth; this time, she chews them well. The chewed cuds pass into the third and fourth stomachs; here they are digested and passed to the small intestine. Blood absorbs nutrients from the digested food and carries them to the udder, where they are made into milk.

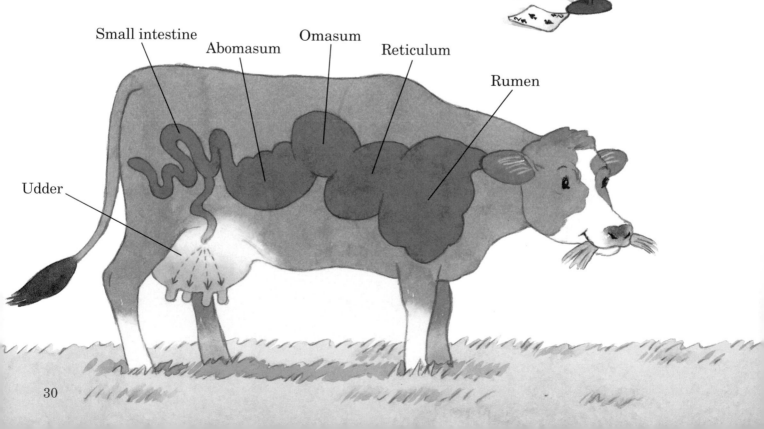

Small intestine　Abomasum　Omasum　Reticulum　Rumen

Udder

◄ Farmers milk their cows twice a day with a milking machine. It has four soft rubber cups that fit onto the cow's nipples, or teats. These cups pump the milk out of the udder and into a tank.

▲ Milk builds up pressure in the udder, so a cow feels terrific after she is milked. A refrigerated tanker (*above*) takes the milk to a dairy, where it is cleaned and put into bottles or cartons. Some milk is made into butter, cheese, or yogurt.

● **To the Parent**

At the dairy, raw milk is tested for fat content, flavor, and bacteria. The milk is then pasteurized, a process that kills germs and extends shelf life. Pasteurization involves heating the milk rapidly, keeping it hot for 16 seconds, then cooling it quickly. Most milk is also homogenized, which breaks the fat into tiny particles so it won't rise to the top.

31

How Is Ice Cream Made?

ANSWER In a factory or at home, there are three basic steps to making ice cream. First, cream, sugar, and flavorings are mixed together. Second, the mixture is whipped. This beats in tiny air bubbles, which make the ice cream light. Third, the mixture is frozen quickly, so that it will be smooth instead of grainy.

■ Turn, turn, turn

Turning the paddle of an ice-cream maker beats air into the ice cream. It also keeps large ice crystals from forming. Adding salt to the ice around the mixture speeds up the freezing process. Can you guess why?

TRY THIS

■ Yum, yum!

Even if you don't have an ice-cream maker, you can still make ice cream at home. This recipe uses plastic zip-type bags. Shaking the bag mixes air into the ice cream. Here's what you need:

½ cup heavy cream
1 tablespoon sugar
¼ teaspoon vanilla
6 tablespoons salt
about 30 small ice cubes
1 pint-size zip-type bag
1 gallon-size zip-type bag

▲ Fill large bag half-full of ice. Add the salt. Put the cream, sugar, and vanilla in small bag and seal it.

▲ Put small bag in big bag; seal. Shake until the mixture looks like ice cream—about five minutes.

▲ Take small bag out of big bag. Wipe off the top and open. Eat out of the bag, or serve in bowls. Enjoy!

❓ Who Invented the Ice-Cream Cone?

The ice-cream cone was invented at the 1904 World's Fair in St. Louis. One day, a waffle maker saw that the ice-cream seller next to him had run out of dishes. He rolled a waffle into a cone and had the man fill it with ice cream. The ice-cream cone was an instant hit.

MINI-DATA

■ Ice-cream bean

Vanilla is the most popular flavor for ice cream. It comes from the seed pods, or beans, of a tropical plant *(right)*. After the beans are picked, they are dried *(below)*, then fermented to release their delicious smell and flavor.

● To the Parent

If air was not beaten into ice cream, it would be too hard—more like frozen milk. Adding salt to the ice in the outside canister of an ice-cream maker lowers the freezing point of water to about 23 degrees F.—cold enough to freeze the cream into tiny ice crystals. Ice-cream manufacturers use huge machines to mix and freeze this chilly treat.

? What Was a Peanut-Butter-and-Jelly Sandwich Before It Got to the Table?

ANSWER You can buy the three ingredients of a PB&J sandwich at the supermarket, but that's not where they start out. Each item—bread, peanut butter, and jelly—begins as a plant grown on a farm. They all make a stop at a factory before being delivered to stores.

▼ **Peanut butter**
Peanuts are seeds that grow underground. They are plowed up in the fall, then taken in trucks to a factory.

▼ At the factory, the peanuts are roasted and shelled. A machine then crushes the roasted nuts into peanut butter. Another machine squirts the butter into jars.

◄ Grape jelly

Grapes grow in bunches. The grapes are skinned and seeded, then mixed with sugar and cooked in big kettles until the jelly thickens. Last, the jelly is pumped into jars.

◄ Bread

1. Bread is made from wheat, a grain that is grown in fields. After the wheat is cut down, or harvested, its seeds are ground into flour at a factory called a mill.

▲ 2. The flour is taken to a bakery. A machine mixes the flour with water and yeast. The yeast makes the dough rise, or get bigger.

▼ 3. The bread dough is divided into loaves and put in pans. Conveyor belts move the pans through an oven, which bakes them. The loaves of bread come out on the other side, where they are sliced and wrapped.

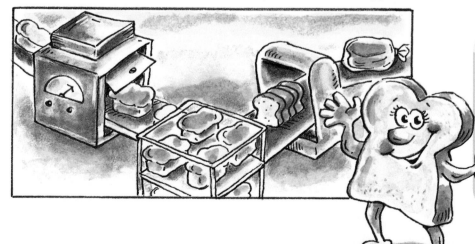

● To the Parent

No one knows who made the first peanut butter. More than 500 years ago, however, people in Africa were grinding peanuts into stews. And people in China have eaten creamy peanut sauces for centuries. Peanut butter was introduced to the U.S. in the late 1800s. Today, some peanut butters have sugar, salt, and oil mixed in with the peanuts.

Where Does Spaghetti Come From?

ANSWER The name "spaghetti" comes from the Italian word for "string." Spaghetti is a kind of pasta, a food made from flour and water. Until about 100 years ago, pasta makers in Naples, Italy, made spaghetti right on the street. They used a wooden screw press, shown below, to push the pasta dough through tiny holes. The long strings were then hung to dry in the sun.

■ Fast food

Italian pasta makers sold dry spaghetti from stalls in the streets. They also cooked the spaghetti in big pots, then sold the hot noodles to people passing by.

 ◄ **Rotini**

 ◄ **Wagon wheel**

 ◄ **Shell**

 ◄ **Cavatappi**

 ◄ **Farfalle (Bow tie)**

 ◄ **Lumache**

◄ **Raviolini**

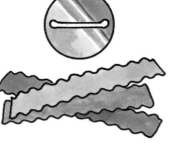

■ Noodle noggin

This funny face shows just seven of the more than 100 shapes in which pasta is sold. Each shape is made by forcing pasta dough through metal molds called dies.

CHECK IT OUT

■ Pasta perfect

▲ Wagon wheels get their spin from a wheel-shaped die.

▲ Lasagne noodles are pressed through a slot with raised ends.

▲ Rotini, or spirals, are squeezed through a squiggly slot.

❓ Why Is a Soft Drink Bubbly?

ANSWER Those little bubbles that fizz up and tickle your nose when you sip a soft drink are made of carbon dioxide. Carbon dioxide is a gas. You can't see it, smell it, or taste it, but it's in the air you breathe. It's also in the cola you drink. That's because the bottling company pumps it into drinks at a factory. The cans or bottles are then quickly sealed, trapping the gas inside until you open the soda: Pssht!

■ Hard work to make a soft drink

Mixing tank

◀ Sugar and special flavorings are mixed with water in a big tank. Every soft-drink company has its own secret recipe.

Carbo-cooler

Filling machine

▲ Carbon dioxide is pumped into the sweet liquid in a big, round refrigerator called a carbo-cooler. The carbon dioxide gives the drink its bright, tingly taste.

■ Make-a-cola

Regular soft drinks are about 90 percent water, and diet soft drinks are 99 percent water. The rest is mostly sweetener, with a little flavoring such as lemon or vanilla. Try this recipe to create your own!

1 cup cold seltzer or club soda
1 teaspoon lemon juice
1 teaspoon vanilla
⅛ teaspoon cinnamon
2 to 3 tablespoons sugar or corn syrup
red, yellow, and green food coloring

Mix the seltzer with the lemon juice, vanilla, cinnamon, and sugar or syrup. Add a few drops of food coloring to turn the liquid brown. Taste the drink. Experiment with the flavorings until the liquid tastes like cola.

▼ The cans move off the conveyor belt and are packed 24 to a case. After that, the cases are loaded on trucks and delivered to stores or vending machines.

Capper

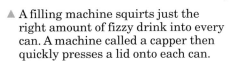

▲ A filling machine squirts just the right amount of fizzy drink into every can. A machine called a capper then quickly presses a lid onto each can.

● **To the Parent**

In 1772, British scientist Joseph Priestley found a way to make artificial mineral water by adding carbon-dioxide gas to water. Carbonated beverages were soon being mass-produced and sold as health tonics. In the mid-1800s, sugar and flavorings were added to the fizzy water, which became the forerunner of the drink we call soda pop.

What Makes Popcorn Pop?

ANSWER Popcorn kernels seem dry, but inside each one is a little bit of water. When a kernel of popcorn is heated, the water in it turns to steam. The trapped steam expands, building up pressure until it bursts through the kernel's hard shell. That's when the kernel explodes with a "Pop!"

In addition to water, popcorn contains protein and starch. When a kernel pops, the protein and starch turn white and fluffy. They also puff up so much they turn the kernel inside out.

40

■ A corny tale

Native Americans discovered popcorn. Some-times they popped it by throwing handfuls into the fire. According to Indian legend, a little man lives inside each kernel. When you heat up his house, he gets so mad he blows up—and that's why popcorn pops!

TRY THIS

■ Hey, bud—it's time to grow!

Did you know that a popcorn kernel is a seed? Inside it is a tiny popcorn plant, which uses the starch and protein in the kernel as food to grow on. Follow these steps to sprout popcorn seeds yourself.

▲ 1. Line a pan with paper towels. Spread popcorn ker-nels in the bottom and moisten the towels with water.

▲ 2. Cover the pan with clear plastic. Put it in a warm, well-lit place.

▲ 3. In a few days, the seeds should grow roots and stems.

● **To the Parent**

Popcorn, a special breed of corn, expands to 30 to 40 times its origi-nal size when heated. Dried pop-corn contains 13 to 14 percent wa-ter. A kernel soaked in water will absorb enough additional moisture to dissolve the food—mainly starch—stored inside it. The living plant in the kernel uses this dis-solved food to start growing.

? Does Chocolate Grow on Trees?

ANSWER This may sound like a sweet dream, but the most important ingredient in chocolate really does grow on trees! Chocolate is made from cacao beans, the seeds of the cacao tree. Cacao trees grow in warm places near the equator in South America, Africa, and Southeast Asia.

◄ **Cacao tree**

▼ **Cacao pod**
The brightly colored seed pods of the cacao tree grow from its main trunk. Inside each pod are about 40 almond-shaped cacao beans.

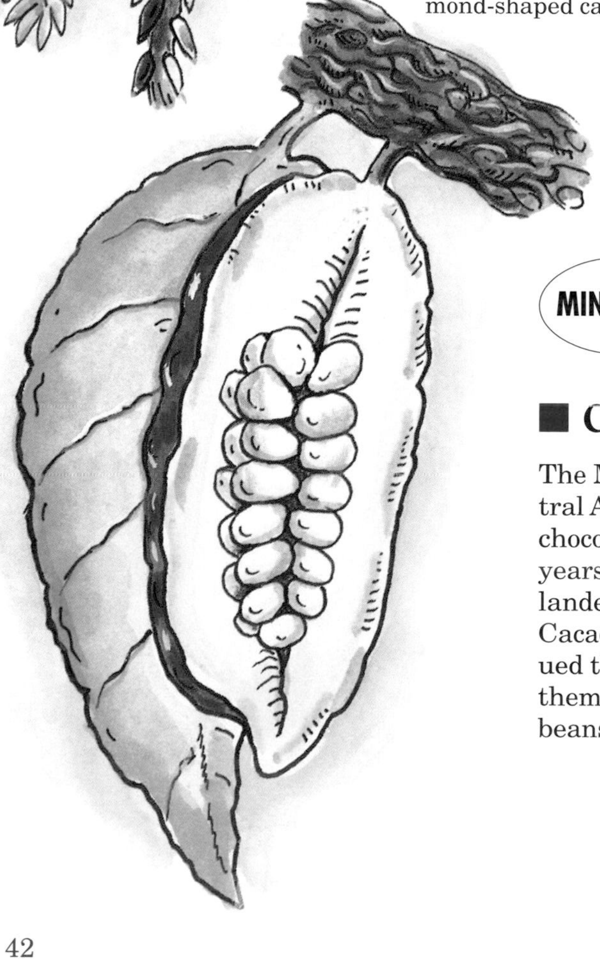

MINI-DATA

■ **Chocolate coins**
The Maya people of Central America enjoyed chocolate at least 1,000 years before Europeans landed on their shores. Cacao beans were so valued that the Maya used them as money. Eight beans bought one rabbit.

42

How Are Candy Bars Made?

▲ 1. A chocolate candy bar starts with a cacao tree. Ripe seed pods are cut off the tree and split open. The cacao beans are removed and spread out to dry in the sun.

▲ 2. The dried cacao beans are put in sacks and loaded on ships. These cargo ships take the beans to Europe or North America, where most chocolate factories are located.

▲ 3. At the factory, the cacao beans are roasted in large ovens. The shells are removed, and the beans are ground into a thick paste called chocolate liquor.

▲ 4. Sugar, milk, and vanilla are added to the chocolate liquor. The mixture is then stirred for three to four days. The longer it's mixed, the better the chocolate!

▲ 5. When the chocolate mixture is super smooth, it is poured into molds. Most candy bars are rectangular, but molds can be any shape. After the chocolate hardens in the molds, it is removed and wrapped for you to eat.

? How Is Glass Made?

ANSWER Glass is a mixture of sand, lime (powdered rock), and soda ash. They are melted together, then allowed to harden. Many glass products, such as cups and bottles, are made by pressing melted glass into molds *(below)*. The oldest way of making glass is glassblowing *(opposite),* in which a glass object is shaped by hand.

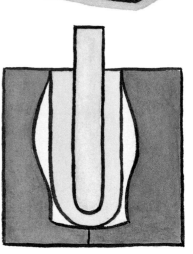

■ From glob to glass

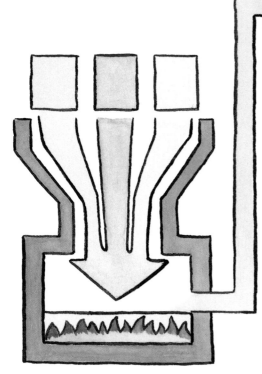

▲ 1. In a furnace, sand, lime, and soda ash are mixed together at extremely high heat—more than 2,500 degrees F. The melted mixture is known as molten glass.

▲ 2. A glob of molten glass is dropped into a bottle-shaped mold, which is made of iron.

▲ 3. A metal plunger pushes the glass down into the mold. The glass begins to fill the mold, taking the shape of a bottle.

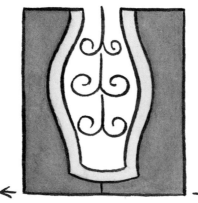

▲ 4. A blast of hot air forces the molten glass into every part of the mold. The glass is then cooled until it can hold its shape.

▲ 5. The mold is split in two and removed. The finished glass bottle is allowed to cool completely.

■ Glassblowing

A glassblower *(left)* uses simple tools to create works of art like the goblet above. First, she attaches a glob of molten glass to one end of a hollow tube. Next, she blows into the other end and turns the tube to shape the glass. Other handblown pieces make up the stem.

■ Stained glass

Artists use dyes to make "stained" glass such as the panes in the window at left (part of a house built in Massachusetts in 1897). Stained glass is also found in church windows. Its colors are brightest when sunlight shines through the glass.

● **To the Parent**

Glass, normally thought of as a solid, often behaves like a liquid. One of the characteristics of a solid—a regular, repeating arrangement of atoms—is absent from glass, whose atoms are arrayed in the haphazard pattern typical of a liquid. This explains why, over time, glass tends to flow. Thus the windows of a very old house are often thicker at the bottom than at the top. To distinguish glass from regular solids, scientists classify it as an "amorphous solid."

45

? Where Does Sand Come From?

ANSWER Sand covers beaches all over the world, but most grains of sand start out as rocks. The rocks fall into rivers and move downstream, getting smaller and smaller until they reach the sea. Sand is made from many different types of rocks, so the sand in one part of the world may look nothing like the sand from somewhere else.

▶ Wind, water, and ice loosen rocks from mountains. Over time, the rocks are washed downhill into rivers. Along the way, they slowly break down into pebbles and sand grains.

Some of the sand grains are deposited on the banks of a river. Others are swept downstream to a lake or an ocean.

Ocean

By the time sand reaches an ocean beach—the trip takes millions of years—it has been smoothed and polished by tumbling and by chemicals in the water.

❓ Does All Sand Look Alike?

▼ The sand grains on Cleopatra's Beach, Turkey *(left)*, are called oolites (magnified 7x, below). Constant wave action has made them smooth and round.

▼ Some sand, like the sample below from a Florida beach, contains the shells of tiny sea creatures that washed ashore and mixed with the sand.

▼ Exploding volcanoes created some of Hawaii's beaches. They threw out molten black rock that was eroded into sand by the action of wind and water.

● **To the Parent**

To most people, the word "sand" denotes any small particle of rock. To geologists, however, the term has a very specific meaning. They use it to describe rock particles measuring .05 to 2 millimeters (.0002 to .008 inches) across. Anything smaller is referred to as silt; anything larger is dubbed gravel.

? Are Seashells Alive?

(ANSWER) Shells aren't alive—but the creatures inside them may be! A seashell is made of a hard, nonliving material that protects the animal living inside it. Clam and oyster shells, for example, are made from the mineral calcium; the animals take it from the seawater around them. Other shellfish, such as crabs and lobsters, make their shells from chitin, a protein they produce themselves.

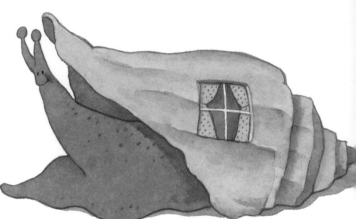

▲ Of the 100,000 animal species that live in shells, the snail *(above)* is one of the best-known.

■ Have you found any of these?

▼ Clam

▼ Moon snail

▲ Pen

Jingle shell

◄ Scallop

◄ Periwinkle

◄ Whelk

▶ Cockle

■ Clamming up

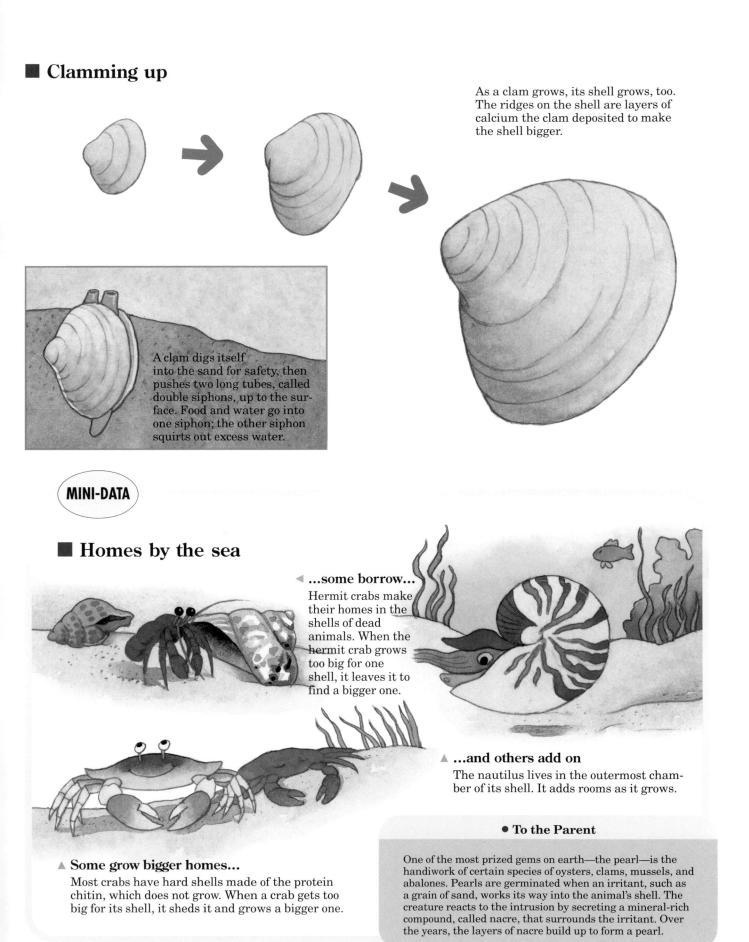

As a clam grows, its shell grows, too. The ridges on the shell are layers of calcium the clam deposited to make the shell bigger.

A clam digs itself into the sand for safety, then pushes two long tubes, called double siphons, up to the surface. Food and water go into one siphon; the other siphon squirts out excess water.

MINI-DATA

■ Homes by the sea

◄ **...some borrow...**
Hermit crabs make their homes in the shells of dead animals. When the hermit crab grows too big for one shell, it leaves it to find a bigger one.

▲ **...and others add on**
The nautilus lives in the outermost chamber of its shell. It adds rooms as it grows.

▲ **Some grow bigger homes...**
Most crabs have hard shells made of the protein chitin, which does not grow. When a crab gets too big for its shell, it sheds it and grows a bigger one.

● **To the Parent**

One of the most prized gems on earth—the pearl—is the handiwork of certain species of oysters, clams, mussels, and abalones. Pearls are germinated when an irritant, such as a grain of sand, works its way into the animal's shell. The creature reacts to the intrusion by secreting a mineral-rich compound, called nacre, that surrounds the irritant. Over the years, the layers of nacre build up to form a pearl.

❓ What Are Clouds?

ANSWER Clouds are clumps of water in the sky. When moist air near the ground gets warm, it rises. This air cools off as it climbs, losing its ability to hold the water vapor it contains. The water vapor condenses, or gloms together, to form larger water droplets. If the air cools enough, the droplets fall to Earth as rain.

■ All steamed up

The birth of a cloud is shown in the steps below. As air near the ground is heated by the earth, it rises. Water vapor it contains condenses to form a cloud.

▲ When the sun heats the ground, a pocket of air above a warm spot begins to rise.

▲ As the pocket keeps rising, its water vapor cools off and condenses, forming a cluster of water droplets.

▲ More warm air feeds the cloud. It may drop its water as rain or snow. If no more air rises, the cloud dissipates.

■ A field guide to clouds

Did you know that scientists have classified 27 different kinds of clouds? The three most common types are pictured here.

▲ **Pillows in the sky**
Low, gray pillows that seem to hover just above the ground are called stratus clouds. They often produce a light drizzle.

▲ **Flying vegetables**
Cumulus clouds—also called fair-weather clouds—look like heads of cauliflower. They can grow into towering cumulonimbus clouds, meaning rain is on the way.

▲ **Winged horses**
Cirrus clouds, sometimes called mare's tails, form high in the atmosphere as their water vapor freezes into ice crystals. The wind then blows the crystals across the sky in long, wispy streaks.

TRY THIS

■ Condensation close up

You can see how a cloud forms—right in your kitchen! Ask an adult to hold a cool metal spoon in steam from a kettle; water droplets will condense on the spoon, just as they do in the air. When the hot steam hits the cold spoon, it turns from a gas to a liquid. The same thing happens when water vapor in warm air hits cooler air and turns to water droplets, making a cloud.

● **To the Parent**

Lightning occurs when an electrical charge builds up in a cloud. If enough charge accumulates, electricity may jump from the cloud to the ground below. A bolt of lightning reaches 50,000 degrees F.—hotter than the surface of the sun.

Where Do Rubber Balls Come From?

(ANSWER) Rubber starts out as latex, a sticky white liquid found in rubber trees. Workers cut a hole in the bark and let the latex drip out. Next, chemicals are added to the latex to make raw rubber. In a factory, the raw rubber is molded into shape, then treated with heat and sulfur to make it strong and stretchy.

▶ 1. A worker "taps," or drains, a rubber tree by pushing a metal spout into the bark and letting latex drip out. A single rubber tree can produce 4 to 15 pounds of latex per year for up to 30 years.

▲ 2. A worker on a rubber plantation stirs acid into freshly tapped latex to coagulate, or join together, its rubber particles.

4. The dry rubber is sent to a factory, where molds called dies press it into shapes you can play with, like the big red ball below.

▲ 3. The coagulated rubber is treated with castor oil and crushed between rollers. It is then washed, dried, and pressed into a bale (above).

Where Did Rubber Get Its Name?

English scientist Joseph Priestley *(below)* is famous for discovering oxygen in 1774, but four years earlier he found out something cool about hardened latex: It could rub away pencil marks! Priestley decided to call this new material "rubber."

■ What's that stuff?

On a voyage to Haiti in 1496, Christopher Columbus watched some boys playing catch with a heavy ball made from the gum of a tree. To the explorer's surprise, the ball could be bounced. Columbus was probably the first European to see rubber in use.

● **To the Parent**

Rubber was not a valuable resource until Charles Goodyear invented vulcanization in 1839. This process, in which rubber is treated with sulfur and heat, keeps rubber from breaking when cold or getting sticky when hot. Vulcanization makes rubber stronger, more elastic, more durable, and more resistant to temperature changes.

Where Did In-Line Skates Come From?

ANSWER The idea for in-line skates got started about 2,000 years ago, when people first began to ice skate. Ice skates could be used only on frozen water, however, and only in the winter. So inventors came up with roller skates, which let people skate on dry land at any time of year. In the 1980s, roller skates gave way to in-line skates, which are easier to use.

▲ **The hit of the party**

Joseph Merlin, a Belgian musician, showed off his homemade skates at a costume party in 1760. But the skates could not be turned, so Merlin crashed into a mirror in the ballroom.

▲ **Hooked on skating**

The first in-line skate was made in 1823! That's the year English inventor Robert Tyers put five wheels in a line on a skate, with a larger one for turning and a front hook for a brake.

▶ **Skates get rolling**

In 1863, U.S. inventor James Plimpton came up with a four-wheeled skate. It could turn without being lifted, allowing roller skaters to move like ice skaters. Roller-skating caught on around the world.

■ Taking it to the streets

In 1980, two brothers from Minnesota who wanted to play hockey off the ice began tinkering with in-line skates. Working in their basement, they started a company called Rollerblade, Inc.

◀ The key to a smooth roll

If you could open up the wheel hub of an in-line skate, you would find seven small metal balls, called bearings, packed in lubricating grease. The bearings rotate in place at high speed, letting the wheels turn quickly and smoothly.

● To the Parent

As of 1997, more than six million people had taken up in-line skating in the United States alone. If your child is one of them, make sure his or her skates have a stiff outer shell for ankle support and a comfortable inner lining. No skater should be without a helmet, wrist guards, and knee and elbow pads.

How Is a Bicycle Made?

ANSWER People all over the world make it possible for you to ride your bike around the block! Some workers build the bike's components, or parts (there are more than 300). Others put the parts together and make sure the bike is safe for you to ride.

■ Where in the world?

Bike parts are manufactured in many different nations, then shipped to a factory to be assembled. Here are some major components and the countries where they are often made:

Frame: United States
Brakes and gears: Japan
Pedals and handlebars: Taiwan
Saddle: Italy
Tires: Germany
Spokes: Switzerland
Tire rims and hubs: France

■ In the factory

◄ **Suitable for framing**
A welder creates the bike frame: Using a flame torch, he melts together strong metal tubes that weigh very little. The frame is then painted.

◄ **The spokes person**
Another worker connects the hub (the center of the wheel) to its outer rim using thin metal spokes. These rigid wires make the wheel strong but light.

► **Don't forget the chain, gang!**
Other workers add to the frame the chain rings, crank arms, rear wheel, and—most important—a chain. The partly assembled bike is then put in a box and sent to a store.

■ At the store

◄ **A bicycle built for you**
Bike mechanics need 18 different tools—but only one hour—to finish assembling the bicycle at the store. They adjust the height of the seat and the handlebars to fit you. Don't forget to wear a helmet!

● **To the Parent**

With 800 million bicycles in circulation, the world's two-wheelers outnumber cars by a ratio of 2 to 1. If you ride with your child, be a model of bicycle safety by wearing a helmet without exception. Insist that younger cyclists do likewise; helmets reduce the risk of head injury by 85 percent.

What's So Fantastic about Plastic?

ANSWER Plastic is strong, light, durable, and reusable. Some plastic items—the water bottle on your bike, for example—are soft and flexible. Others, like the outer shell of your bike helmet, are hard and rigid. The main part of the helmet is made of a plastic called polystyrene, which absorbs the impact of a crash—and keeps your brains from getting scrambled!

■ How plastic is made

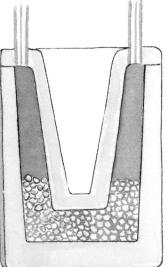

▲ A Styrofoam cup starts out as polystyrene pellets *(above)*. Polystyrene is made by mixing ethylene, a gas, with benzene, a light oil that comes from petroleum.

▽ 1. To begin making the foam cup, the beads are placed in a mold.

▽ 2. Next, steam is forced into the mold. This causes the beads to swell up like tiny balloons.

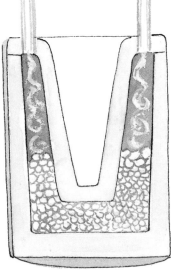

▽ 3. As the beads expand, they fill the mold and attach themselves to one another.

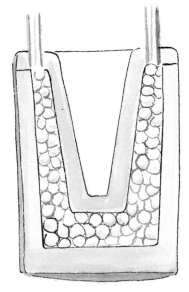

▶ 4. The finished product—a polystyrene cup—keeps hot drinks from cooling off and cold drinks from heating up.

 # What Is Plastic Used For?

You may be surprised to learn how many ordinary objects are made of plastic. In the picture below, for example, 11 things outdoors are at least partly plastic. Inside, 21 things are made of plastic, or have plastic components. Can you spot them all? The answers appear below.

▲ Plastic that can be reused has a number that tells the recycling center how to sort it. Eighty-eight percent of recycled plastics are marked with a 1 or a 2.

CHECK IT OUT

■ Polartec

Polartec is a material made from recycled soft-drink bottles. The bottles are changed into plastic pellets, which are spun into threads and woven into clothing.

● **To the Parent**

Recycling plastics is common—but far from universal. In 1995, 41 percent of plastic soft-drink bottles—but only 22 percent of plastic bottles used for milk, shampoo, and detergents—were recycled. Be prepared for your kids to lead the way in family efforts to recycle; help them by providing separate receptacles for "trash" made of glass, paper, plastic, and cardboard.

Outdoors: slide, swing seat, window, siding on house, eyeglasses, chairs, table, drinking cups, tricycle, bottle, planter. Inside: clock, wallpaper, telephone, sofa, blinds, window, radio, soda bottle, cups, table, chair, purse, sandals, carpeting, blocks, truck, rocking animal, television, VCR, dog bowl, dog bone.

How Do Light Bulbs Work?

Filament

ANSWER A light bulb turns electricity into light. In an incandescent bulb (the most common kind), a thin wire called a filament is heated to a bright glow that creates light. In a fluorescent bulb, electricity sparks a chain reaction among the chemicals in a glass tube, causing them to fluoresce, or throw off light.

■ A coil to see by

When you turn on an incandescent bulb, electricity flows through a tightly wound metal thread called a filament. The filament is made of tungsten, which becomes glowing hot—4,500 degrees F.—in less than a second. This glow supplies light.

Connecting and supporting wire

Glass support

Base

◄ A filament is about two feet long *(left)*. To fit inside a light bulb, it must be wrapped around another wire. Longer, thicker filaments increase the bulb's power.

■ Bright light from a dim bulb

The bulb in a car headlight is just 55 watts—weaker than a desk lamp. It throws a powerful light, however, because it is backed by a concave mirror (a mirror shaped like the inside of a cereal bowl). Light leaves the bulb in all directions, but the mirror reflects the light forward as a single, narrow beam.

Mirror

Bulb

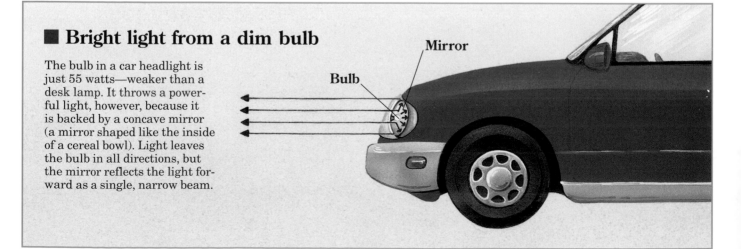

■ Ready...set...glow!

▶ Flipping the switch of a fluorescent light sends current to an electrode—a small wire coil—at each end of a long glass bulb. The electrodes shoot out tiny particles called electrons.

▶ The electrons hit atoms of mercury gas floating inside the bulb. These collisions energize the mercury atoms, bumping them up to a higher activity level.

▶ The mercury atoms release their energy as waves of ultraviolet light. These waves hit phosphor molecules lining the inside of the bulb. As the phosphors get energized, they release their energy in the form of visible light.

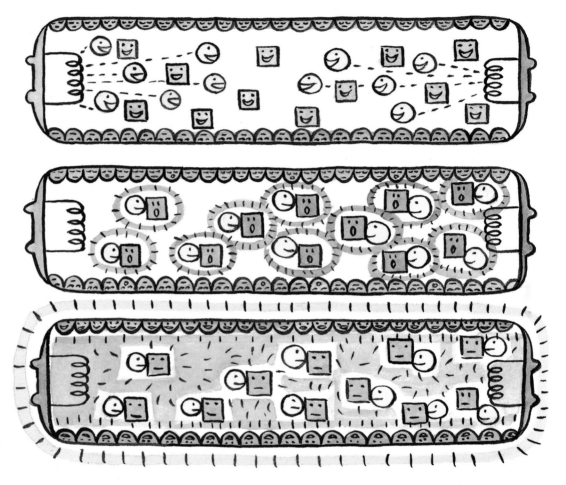

■ Viva Las Vegas!

Did this palm tree catch your eye? That's because it's made of bright neon lights. A neon light contains neon gas, not mercury gas. When the light is turned on, the neon atoms release energy in the form of red light. To produce blue or green light, a bulb containing a different gas—argon—must be used.

How Is Money Manufactured?

ANSWER There are two kinds of money. Coins are struck, or stamped, on metal. Bills are printed on paper. At one time, coins were made of gold or silver. Today they are made of less valuable metals, such as copper and nickel, because gold and silver became worth much more than the face value of the coins. The methods used to manufacture money are shown below.

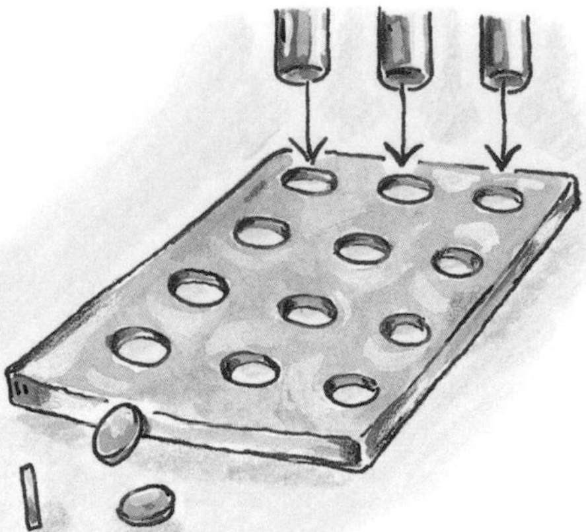

▲ **A blanket of blanks**

A thin sheet of metal is fed through a machine that punches out round shapes, called "blanks."

▲ **Heads *and* tails**

After a second machine adds a raised edge to the blanks, a steel press *(above)* strikes both sides of each blank to complete the coins.

■ **Drawn and quartered**

Guided by a design, a sculptor-engraver carves a large-scale model of a coin. A reducing machine traces the design at actual size onto a steel blank. This blank, called the master hub, is used to make the dies, or metal stamps, that strike the coins.

◄ **Die**

■ Cool coins from all over

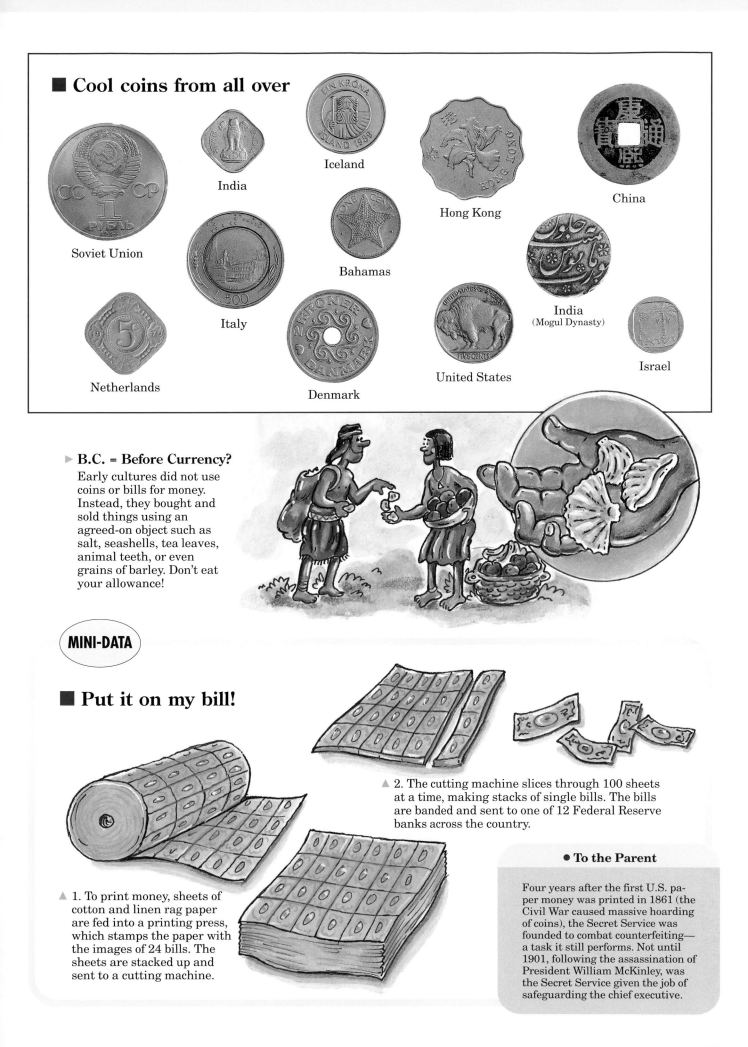

Iceland

India

Soviet Union

Hong Kong

China

Bahamas

Italy

India
(Mogul Dynasty)

Netherlands

Denmark

United States

Israel

► B.C. = Before Currency?

Early cultures did not use coins or bills for money. Instead, they bought and sold things using an agreed-on object such as salt, seashells, tea leaves, animal teeth, or even grains of barley. Don't eat your allowance!

MINI-DATA

■ Put it on my bill!

▲ 2. The cutting machine slices through 100 sheets at a time, making stacks of single bills. The bills are banded and sent to one of 12 Federal Reserve banks across the country.

▲ 1. To print money, sheets of cotton and linen rag paper are fed into a printing press, which stamps the paper with the images of 24 bills. The sheets are stacked up and sent to a cutting machine.

● To the Parent

Four years after the first U.S. paper money was printed in 1861 (the Civil War caused massive hoarding of coins), the Secret Service was founded to combat counterfeiting—a task it still performs. Not until 1901, following the assassination of President William McKinley, was the Secret Service given the job of safeguarding the chief executive.

Where Do Diamonds Come From?

ANSWER Diamonds are beautiful gems—and the hardest minerals on earth. They are created 60 to 95 miles beneath the surface of the planet, where high heat and pressure squash carbon into diamond crystals. (In its soft form, carbon is part of the graphite in pencils.) Small fake diamonds can be made in a lab, but only the earth creates large, gem-quality diamonds.

■ Buried treasures

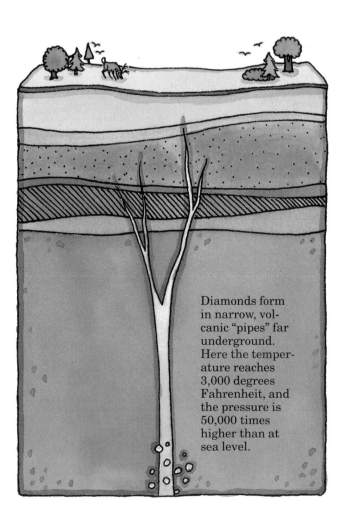

Diamonds form in narrow, volcanic "pipes" far underground. Here the temperature reaches 3,000 degrees Fahrenheit, and the pressure is 50,000 times higher than at sea level.

Gas in the pipe explodes, shooting melted rock up toward the surface. This molten rock, called magma, carries the diamonds with it.

■ The Hope diamond

▲ At 9.1 grams, the Hope diamond is the largest blue-tinged diamond in the world. A jeweler donated it to the Smithsonian Institution in 1958.

▲ At the surface, the magma cools and turns hard. Miners dig down through the now-solid rock to get at the diamonds.

■ From stone to gem

Here's how skilled craftspeople turn raw diamonds into the bright gems used in jewelry:

▶ When found, a diamond may look like any other rock. It may be shiny or dull.

◀ Rough diamonds usually have eight sides and form a double pyramid.

▶ Part of the top pyramid is removed by sawing the diamond in two.

◀ The diamond is rounded off by spinning it beside a second diamond.

▶ Cutters grind facets, or faces, on the diamond. Most finished diamonds have 58 facets.

◀ Mounted in a ring, the finished diamond has a rainbow-colored sparkle.

● To the Parent

Diamonds are made of the same chemical element as the graphite used for pencil lead, but their properties differ radically. Whereas graphite is one of the softest minerals, diamond is unarguably the hardest. This is because the carbon atoms in graphite arrange themselves in sheets that are only loosely bonded, so the layers slide over each other. In a diamond, by contrast, the carbon atoms are strongly bonded in a compact, three-dimensional lattice.

How Were Some Famous Toys Invented?

ANSWER Some of the most fun toys to play with were invented mainly by accident. The Frisbee got its start when college students put an ordinary pie pan to new use. Other toys, such as Silly Putty and the Slinky, were invented for practical purposes but turned out to be more popular as toys.

■ Silly Putty

▲ Trying to invent synthetic rubber in 1943, engineer James Wright *(above)* made a goo that stretched farther and bounced higher than natural rubber. The goo fascinated businessman Paul Hodgson, who packed it in plastic eggs and began selling it as Silly Putty. Since then, 200 million eggs have sold.

■ The Frisbee

Yale University students of the 1920s played catch with metal pie pans made by the Frisbie Pie Company. (They yelled "Frisbie!" to warn others that a pan was on the way.) In 1948, California carpenter Walter Morrison invented a similar flying disk, the plastic "Pluto Platter." It, too, became popular on college campuses, so the company borrowed the name of the pie pans and renamed it the Frisbee.

The Slinky

Richard James was working at his desk in a Philadelphia shipyard in 1943 when a special spring fell off a shelf and "walked" end over end down the shelves and onto the floor. James realized that the spring could be made into a toy. He showed it to his wife, Betty, who named it the Slinky. After selling 400 Slinkys in one night at Gimbels department store, James quit his job and began making Slinkys full-time.

Where Does the Calendar Come From?

ANSWER The modern calendar was adopted in the 1500s to correct the calendar used by the ancient Romans. It has 12 months because the moon goes through 12 cycles in a year. No one knows why a week has seven days. It may be because people knew of only seven planets—including the sun and the moon—in ancient times.

JANUARY

January is named for the Roman god Janus, the two-faced god of beginnings. One face looked back in time; the other faced forward.

FEBRUARY

Februa was a Roman holiday celebrated in the second month of the year, which is now February.

MARCH

The war god Martius—the Roman equivalent of the Greek god Mars—gave March its name.

JULY

July is named for the Roman general Julius Caesar. He lived in the 1st century B.C.

AUGUST

Augustus Caesar was the first Roman emperor. He ruled from 27 B.C. to A.D. 14—and loaned his name to the month of August.

SEPTEMBER

Though it is ninth in the modern calendar, September came seventh in the Roman calendar. The Latin word for "seven" is "septem."

▲ **Gregory XIII**
In the 1500s, Pope Gregory XIII *(above)* asked that the ancient Roman calendar be changed to keep better time. The result, still in use today, is called the Gregorian calendar.

▶ **Monday**
The first day of the week is named after the moon.

▶ **Tuesday**
The second day of the week gets its name from Tiw, the Norse god of war.

Sunday
The last day of the week is named after the sun.

Saturday
Saturday is named after Saturn, which was the most distant planet known to people living in ancient Mesopotamia.

APRIL
The Romans called this month Aprilis—a variation on Aphrodite, the Greek goddess of love and beauty.

MAY
The Roman goddess Maia gave her name to the merry month of May.

JUNE
June comes from the goddess Juno. She was the wife of Jupiter, king of the Roman gods.

Friday
The last day of the work-week is named after Frigga. She was the supreme goddess in Norse myths.

OCTOBER
October was the eighth month in the Roman calendar. Its name comes from "octo," the Latin word for "eight."

NOVEMBER
November, from the Latin word "nove," or nine, came ninth in the Roman calendar.

DECEMBER
December was the 10th month in the Roman calendar. It gets its name from the Latin word for 10, "decem."

Thursday
Thor, the Norse god of thunder, gave his name to Thursday.

Wednesday
The middle day of the school week is named after Wodin, leader of all Norse gods.

● **To the Parent**

The phrase "once in a blue moon" has its origins in the calendar. Traditionally, a blue moon is the name given to the second full moon in any calendar month—an event that occurs only once every few years. Why such a moon should be referred to as "blue," however, remains a mystery.

? How Do Musical Instruments Make Sound?

ANSWER All instruments make music in the same basic way. They produce vibrations in the air, which we hear as sound. If the air vibrates fast, we hear a high note; if it vibrates slowly, the note we hear is low. There are four main groups of instruments: winds, strings, brass, and percussion. The workings of a recorder and a guitar are explained here.

■ Wind instruments

◀ A recorder works like any other wind instrument. When you blow into the mouthpiece, the air inside the tube begins to vibrate. Fast vibrations make high notes; slow vibrations make low ones. The vibration speed is determined by the length of the tube, which changes as the air holes are blocked by the musician's fingers.

Cover just a few holes with your fingers, and the sealed length of the tube is fairly short. This makes the air in the tube vibrate quickly when you blow into the recorder, producing a high note.

Cover a few more holes, and the sealed length of the tube becomes much longer. Now the air vibrates slowly when you blow into the instrument, making a low note.

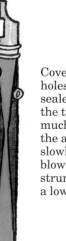

■ String instruments

When you pluck a guitar string, it vibrates. The air around the string vibrates, too. These vibrations are amplified, or made louder, by the hollow body of the guitar. The faster the string vibrates, the higher the note sounds.

Shorter

Longer

▲ A string's vibration speed can be increased by "shortening" the string. This is done by pressing the string against the neck of the guitar. The shorter the string, the higher its note.

TRY THIS

■ Bottles and bands

▲ To make your own wind instruments, fill bottles of the same size with differing amounts of water. Blow across the tops of the bottles to create music. Which bottles produce the highest notes?

▲ Stretch a rubber band between two nails in a board. Press down on the rubber band at various points and pluck it each time to make high and low notes.

● **To the Parent**

Most instruments have hazy origins—but not the saxophone. This woodwind instrument was patented in 1846 by Adolphe Sax, a Belgian instrument maker seeking to improve the clarinet. The saxophone quickly found its way into military bands and has since become a staple of popular music and jazz.

How Does Water Get to My House?

ANSWER Most water that comes straight from rivers and lakes is not safe to drink. It contains germs, dirt, and other tiny particles you cannot see without a microscope. To be made clean enough for drinking and washing, the water is treated, or purified, as shown here.

▲ **Intake**

1. First, water is collected from a lake, a river, or an underground well. Filters strain out fish, plants, insects, and other debris.

▲ **Chemical treatment**

2. Chlorine and lime—chemicals that kill germs—are added to the water. They make the water taste and smell better.

▼ **Sedimentation**

3. The water is stirred up. This makes pieces of dirt stick together. The water is then allowed to stand so these dirty clumps settle out as sediment.

72

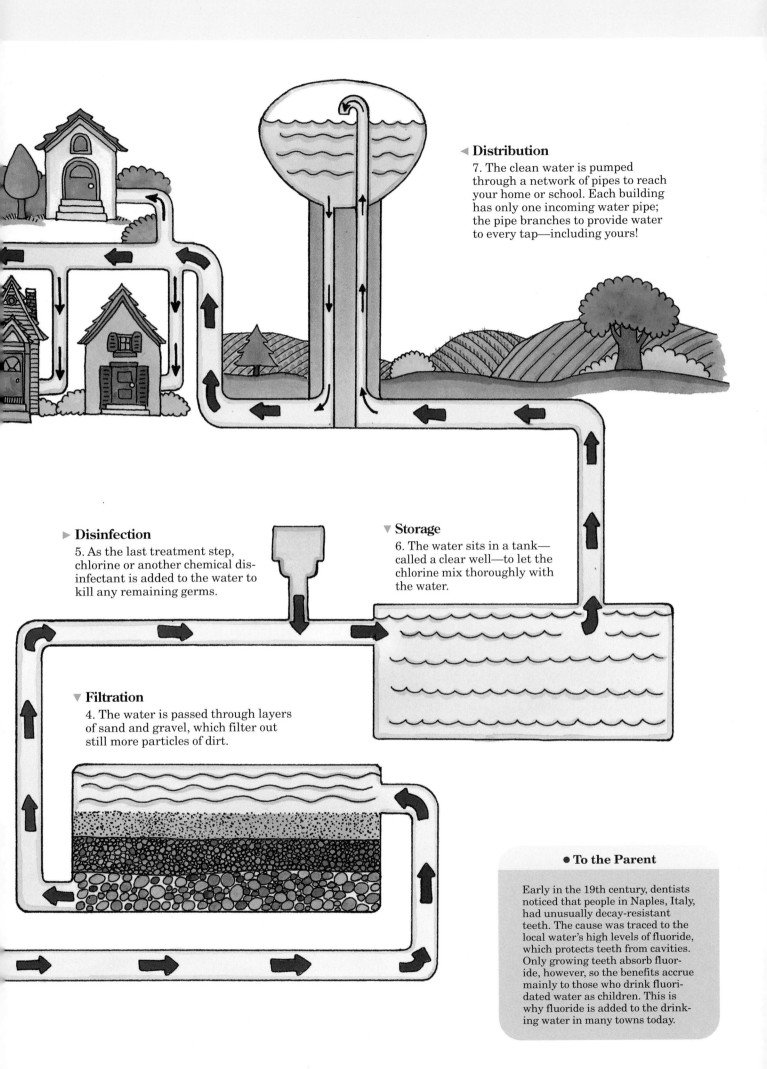

◄ Distribution

7. The clean water is pumped through a network of pipes to reach your home or school. Each building has only one incoming water pipe; the pipe branches to provide water to every tap—including yours!

► Disinfection

5. As the last treatment step, chlorine or another chemical disinfectant is added to the water to kill any remaining germs.

▼ Storage

6. The water sits in a tank—called a clear well—to let the chlorine mix thoroughly with the water.

▼ Filtration

4. The water is passed through layers of sand and gravel, which filter out still more particles of dirt.

● To the Parent

Early in the 19th century, dentists noticed that people in Naples, Italy, had unusually decay-resistant teeth. The cause was traced to the local water's high levels of fluoride, which protects teeth from cavities. Only growing teeth absorb fluoride, however, so the benefits accrue mainly to those who drink fluoridated water as children. This is why fluoride is added to the drinking water in many towns today.

73

How Is Soap Made?

ANSWER Soap is made of fats and of chemicals called bases, which turn the fat molecules into soap molecules. The fats come from animals, such as cows and sheep, or from vegetables, such as coconut and palm. The ingredients are mixed, then pressed into a long bar; this is sliced into small bars that are stamped with the company name.

How Does Soap Work?

Soap may not be your favorite thing, but you can't get clean without it. That's because water alone does not have what it takes to get rid of grease and stains. The drawings below show how molecules of water and soap team up to remove dirt.

◀ Unable to bond with and dissolve the dirt molecules that make up this stain, molecules of water cannot remove the greasy spot.

▶ A molecule of soap has two ends: One end likes to bond with water molecules, but the other end likes to bond with dirt molecules. When soap is added to water, the soap molecules arrange themselves in clusters. The water-loving ends face out; the dirt-loving ends face in.

When they reach a stain, the dirt-loving ends of the soap molecule stick to it and dissolve it. The soap-and-dirt mixture is then carried off by the water.

● To the Parent

Soap often combines with the minerals in tap water to form a solid called soap scum—the familiar "ring" around bathtubs. The same thing happens when soap is used to wash the hair. Shampoo therefore contains special additives, known as builders, that make tap-water minerals nonreactive, preventing the formation of soap scum.

What's in Toothpaste?

ANSWER You wouldn't chew birch trees and seaweed—or would you? Chemicals from both plants are in toothpaste, which also contains abrasives that scrub your teeth and flavors that make the paste taste good. Other ingredients are added to give the toothpaste its consistency and to make it foam up when you start brushing.

■ The secret of your smile

◀ Xylitol
Drawn from birch trees, the chemical called xylitol adds a sweet flavor to toothpaste.

◀ Peppermint oil
Is mint your favorite flavor for toothpaste? The taste comes from peppermint oil, which is squeezed from the leaves of the peppermint plant.

▶ Carrageenan
This substance, found in seaweed, is used to thicken toothpaste.

▲ Water
Most of the ingredients in toothpaste are powders. To make a paste, they must be mixed with water.

▶ Sodium lauryl sulfate
This compound makes toothpaste foam. It comes from coconut oil.

▼ Sodium bicarbonate
This mineral works as an abrasive, or scrubber. It also destroys acids that cause tooth decay.

How Is Toothpaste Made?

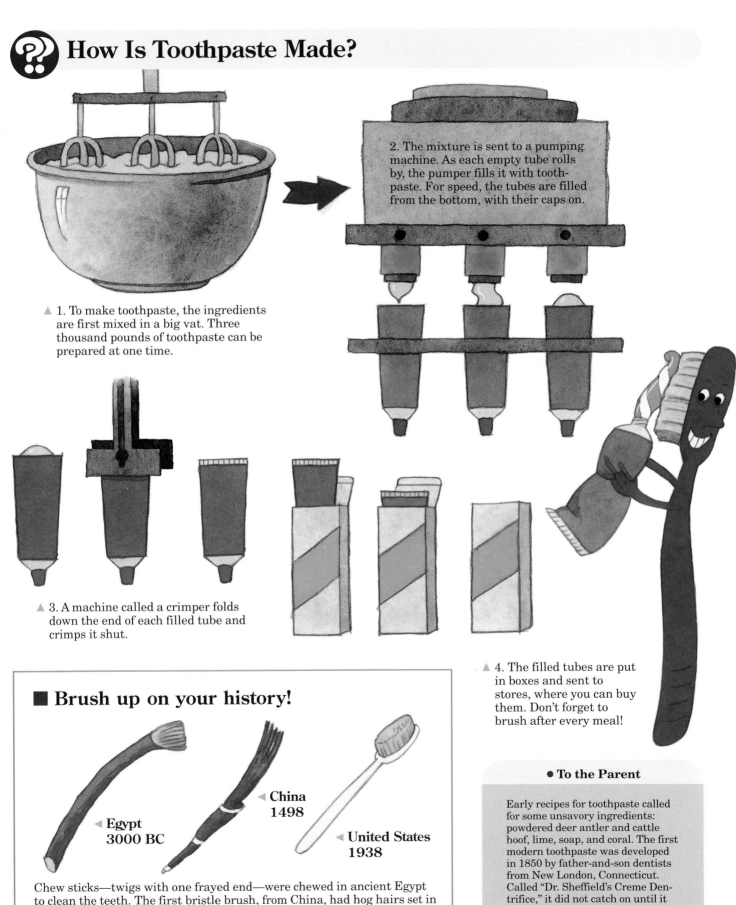

▲ 1. To make toothpaste, the ingredients are first mixed in a big vat. Three thousand pounds of toothpaste can be prepared at one time.

2. The mixture is sent to a pumping machine. As each empty tube rolls by, the pumper fills it with toothpaste. For speed, the tubes are filled from the bottom, with their caps on.

▲ 3. A machine called a crimper folds down the end of each filled tube and crimps it shut.

▲ 4. The filled tubes are put in boxes and sent to stores, where you can buy them. Don't forget to brush after every meal!

■ Brush up on your history!

◄ Egypt
3000 BC

◄ China
1498

◄ United States
1938

Chew sticks—twigs with one frayed end—were chewed in ancient Egypt to clean the teeth. The first bristle brush, from China, had hog hairs set in a bamboo handle. The modern nylon-bristle brush was invented in 1938.

● To the Parent

Early recipes for toothpaste called for some unsavory ingredients: powdered deer antler and cattle hoof, lime, soap, and coral. The first modern toothpaste was developed in 1850 by father-and-son dentists from New London, Connecticut. Called "Dr. Sheffield's Creme Dentrifice," it did not catch on until it was packaged in tin tubes.

❓ How Is a Book Made?

Once upon a time there was a dragon who loved to eat ice cream.

ANSWER It takes many people to turn a good idea into a great book. Some people work for a publishing company, which sells books. They have fun jobs because they get to work with words and pictures all day. When everything is correct, the publisher sends the book to a printing company; the people there make lots of copies of the book.

Once upon a time there was a dragon who couldn't loved to eat ice cream.

▲ **Author**
The writer works long and hard to come up with a good idea and put it down in words. Some book authors write on computers; others use paper and pencil.

▲ **Editor**
An editor works with the writer to make sure the words are clear, the facts are right, and the book is fun and interesting to read.

▶ **Artist**
An artist draws pictures that help tell the story. The pictures bring the book's characters to life. Some artists illustrate books and write them, too.

◀ **Designer**
A designer decides what the book will look like. She figures out the best way to make the words and pictures go together on each page.

78

▲ Printing

The pages are made into film, which is turned into metal printing plates. At the printing company, a machine like the one above inks the plates and presses huge sheets of paper onto them.

▼ Binding

The printed sheets of paper are folded into booklets of 16 or 32 pages. Glue or thread is used to bind the booklets together. The cover of the book is then glued on.

◄ Reading

Publishers sell the printed books to schools, libraries, and stores across the country. The people who work in these places know a lot about books. They can help you find one that's just right for you—but first you have to ask!

MINI-DATA

Yellow   **Cyan**   **Magenta**   **Black**

Did you know that printers use only four colors of ink to print most pictures? One color is printed at a time. When combined, the inks produce enough shades to make a full-color picture book.

Full color

● **To the Parent**

American firms published about 8,000 new children's books—evenly divided between fiction and nonfiction—in 1996. In an average year, Americans buy more than one billion books, spending $1.2 billion on children's books alone. Other readers borrow books from the country's estimated 125,000 libraries. If you or your child has a question or comment about this particular book, please write to the editor, Allan Fallow, at 2000 Duke Street, Alexandria, Virginia, 22314, U.S.A.

What Did These Start Out As?

ANSWER As you have learned, many final products look nothing like the raw materials from which they were made. Can you match each item on the left with its raw material on the right?

▲ **Drinking glass**

▲ **Bicycle tire**

▲ **Silk shirt**

Drinking glass started as sand; bicycle tire started as latex in rubber tree; silk shirt started as silk worms in cocoons.

Growing-Up Album

The Case of the Mixed-Up Animator

On pages 18-19, you saw how animators bring cartoon characters to life. That's what artist Roz Schanzer was doing when she dropped these pictures and got them all mixed up. Can you put them back in the right order?

A _____ _____ _____ _____

B _____ _____ _____ _____

C _____ _____ _____ _____

Answers: A–2,4,1,3; B–3,1,4,2; C–1,3,2,4

Water + Sun = ?

Whether they take place in nature or in a factory, many processes can be thought of as equations, or math problems. Complete the equations below by picking the item from the right that fits in each one.

1

2

3

4

A. broccoli

B. rocks

C. trees

D. cow

E. clouds

F. fire

Animal, Vegetable, or Mineral?

Everyday things often have surprising origins, or beginnings. Try to match the items below with their sources at the bottom of the page. If you're curious about any of the connections, look in your library for a book about it.

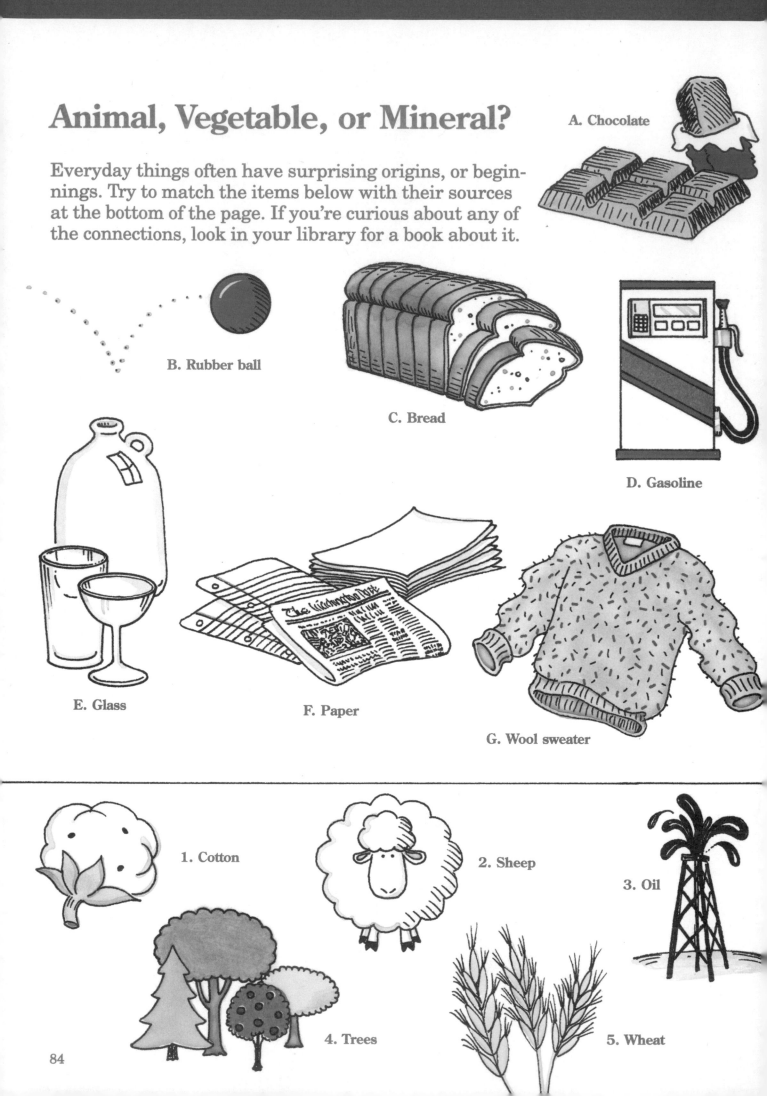

A. Chocolate

B. Rubber ball

C. Bread

D. Gasoline

E. Glass

F. Paper

G. Wool sweater

1. Cotton

2. Sheep

3. Oil

4. Trees

5. Wheat

I. Soap

H. Plastics

J. Polartec clothing

K. Eraser

L. Chalk

M. Blue jeans

N. Cereal

6. Cacao tree

7. Plastics

8. Vegetable oil

9. Rubber tree

10. Limestone

11. Sand

Answers: A-6; B, K-9; C, N-5; D, H-3; E-11; F-4; G-2; I-8; J-7; L-10; M-1.

Build a Bike!

It's the first day of Antonio's new job: working as a mechanic in a bike shop owned by Virginia, a very messy per- son. Virginia left Antonio a list of parts to put together for a new bike. Can you help him find them all?

helmet

2 wheels

frame

chain ring

seat

pedals

fork

chain

freewheel

handlebars

pump

Time-Life Books is a division of Time Life Inc.

TIME LIFE INC.

PRESIDENT and CEO: George Artandi

TIME-LIFE BOOKS

PRESIDENT: John D. Hall
PUBLISHER/MANAGING EDITOR: Neil Kagan

A Child's First Library of Learning
WHERE THINGS COME FROM

EDITOR: Allan Fallow
DIRECTOR, NEW PRODUCT DEVELOPMENT: Elizabeth D. Ward

Deputy Editor: Terrell Smith
Picture Coordinator: Lisa Groseclose
Associate Editor/Research: Mary M. Saxton

Design: Studio A—Antonio Alcalá, Virginia Ibarra-Garza,
Wendy Schleicher, Richard Friend
Special Contributors: Patricia Daniels, Marfé Ferguson Delano, Marike
Estepp, Mark Galan, Colette Stockum, Elizabeth Thompson (research
and writing); Patricia Daniels (text editing); Colette Stockum (copyedit).

Consultants: Jon Eklund is curator of Physical Sciences at the National
Museum of American History, Smithsonian Institution, Washington, D.C.
Marie Jones, of the Network for Excellence in Manufacturing (Ann Arbor, Michigan), provides industrial engineering training to a national network of organizations that assist manufacturers.

Correspondents: Maria Vincenza Aloisi (Paris), Christine Hinze
(London), Christina Lieberman (New York).

Vice President, Director of Finance: Christopher Hearing
Vice President, Book Production: Marjann Caldwell
Director of Photography and Research: John Conrad Weiser
Director of Editorial Administration: Barbara Levitt
Production Manager: Gertraude Schaefer
Quality Assurance Manager: Dominique Fleurima
Library: Louise D. Forstall

Photography: Cover: Roger Foley. Back Cover: Courtesy Tom Barry,
Trek Bicycle Corporation. 1: © Alex Bartel/The Picture Cube. 7: Courtesy Virginia Ibarra-Garza, photographed by Jeff Watts. 10: Binney &
Smith Inc. 11: Shirley Woodford. 13: Courtesy Flights of Fancy, Leamington Spa, Warwickshire—Derek Henley, Flights of Fancy, Leamington
Spa, Warwickshire; The Bentcil Company, Indianapolis, Ind. (3); courtesy
Shirley Grundman; The Bentcil Company, Indianapolis, Ind. (3); all pencils photographed by Jeff Watts. 29: © Dr. Jeremy Burgess/Science Photo Library, Photo Researchers. 33: Photo Courtesy McCormick/Schilling
Spices. 45: The Corning Museum of Glass, Corning, N.Y., no. 51.3.118—
Clara S. Peck Endowment Purchase, The Corning Museum of Glass,
Corning, N.Y. 47: Walter N. Mack. 51: National Oceanic and Atmospheric
Administration, NOAA Photo Section—© Tom Bean/Stockmarket;
NOAA. 52: © Paula Lerner, Woodfin Camp and Associates—The Tun Abdul Razak Research Centre, Hertford, Hertfordshire; © Richard Hutchings, cons.024515/PhotoEdit. 61: © George Obremski/Image Bank.
63: Courtesy Rob Pearson; courtesy Mark Galan; courtesy John Hall;
courtesy Mark Galan; courtesy Barbara M. Sheppard—courtesy the
Weatherley family; courtesy Mark Galan; courtesy Rob Pearson—courtesy Mary E. Carey; courtesy the Weatherley family; courtesy Roman
Richardson III; courtesy Mark Galan, all coins photographed by Jeff
Watts. 65: Courtesy of Smithsonian Institution, Washington, D.C., photo
no. 78-8853. 80: Courtesy Mimi Fallow, photographed by Jeff Watts;
Goodyear—used with permission of Michelin North America, Inc. All
rights reserved; © Joyce Photographics, Photo Researchers—courtesy
Hannah Lesk, photographed by Jeff Watts; courtesy Katherine Weatherley, photographed by Jeff Watts. 81: © Richard Hutchings, Photo Researchers.

Illustrations: **Loel Barr:** 13, 18-19, 34-35, 40, 42-43, 46-47, 53, 62-63,
74-75. **Leila Cabib:** 22 *(top right)*, 23, 38-39, 56 *(top right)*, 57-59.
Richard Friend: 8-9, 29. **Annie Lunsford:** 20-21, 30-31, 48-49, 76-77.
Roz Schanzer: 4-5, 10-11, 26-27, 36-37, 54-55, 64-69, 72-73, 78-79, 82-87.
Carol Schwartz: 12, 14-15, 22 *(bottom)*, 52, 56 *(bottom)*, 60.
Bethann Thornburgh: 6-7, 16-17, 24-25, 28, 32-33, 41, 44-45, 50-51, 61,
70-71. **Stephen Wagner:** front and back cover illustrations.

First printing. Printed in U.S.A.
Published simultaneously in Canada.
School and library distribution by Time-Life Education, P.O. Box 85026,
Richmond, Virginia 23285-5026.

Time Life is a trademark of Time Warner Inc. U.S.A.

Library of Congress Cataloging in Publication Data
Where Things Come From.
    88 pp. 1.4 cm.—(A child's first library of learning)
    Summary: Provides answers to children's questions on a variety of
topics, including "How are sneakers made?" "Where do pictures on TV
come from?" "Are seashells alive?" "How were some famous toys invented?" and "What are clouds?"
    ISBN 0-8094-9484-1
    1. Manufactures—Juvenile literature. [1. Manufactures—Miscellanea. 2. Science—Miscellanea. 3. Questions and answers.] I. Time-Life
Books. II. Series.
TS146.W55 1997
670—dc21   97-3636
                                                                   CIP
                                                                    AC

OTHER PUBLICATIONS:

COOKING	DO IT YOURSELF
Weight Watchers® Smart Choice Recipe Collection	The Time-Life Complete Gardener
Great Taste–Low Fat	Home Repair and Improvement
Williams-Sonoma Kitchen Library	The Art of Woodworking
	Fix It Yourself

TIME-LIFE KIDS	HISTORY
Family Time Bible Stories	The American Story
Library of First Questions and Answers	Voices of the Civil War
A Child's First Library of Learning	The American Indians
I Love Math	Lost Civilizations
Nature Company Discoveries	Mysteries of the Unknown
Understanding Science & Nature	Time Frame
	The Civil War
SCIENCE/NATURE	Cultural Atlas
Voyage Through the Universe	

For information on and a full description of any of the Time-Life Books
series listed above, please call 1-800-621-7026 or write:

Reader Information
Time-Life Customer Service
P.O. Box C-32068
Richmond, Virginia 23261-2068